W e're dealing with a very dangerous woman, Elizabeth. I have to find her."

"You will. You really are amazing at your work."

"Thanks for acknowledging that. But then, so are you."

Recalling the book he had been given at the Promise Keepers meeting, he decided to swallow his pride.

"Elizabeth, I want to apologize to you for…" He broke off, shaking his head. "Where do I start? I really do want to be a better person, Elizabeth. When I can accomplish that, I hope to be a better father…and husband."

Michael walked around the desk and stood beside her. Then, as he stared down at her, something happened between them that neither could have predicted or prevented.

He leaned down, gently planting his lips on hers. "I still love you, Elizabeth. I always will."

Tears filled her eyes. She couldn't speak. She raised on tiptoe to touch her lips to his again. "Me too," she whispered.

Palisades.
Pure Romance.

FICTION THAT FEATURES CREDIBLE CHARACTERS AND

ENTERTAINING PLOT LINES, WHILE CONTINUING TO UPHOLD

STRONG CHRISTIAN VALUES. FROM HIGH ADVENTURE

TO TENDER STORIES OF THE HEART, EACH PALISADES

ROMANCE IS AN UNDILUTED STORY OF LOVE,

FROM BEGINNING TO END!

A PALISADES CONTEMPORARY ROMANCE

PROMISES

Peggy Darty

PALISADES

PROMISES
published by Palisades
a division of Multnomah Publishers, Inc.

© 1997 by Peggy Darty
International Standard Book Number: 1-57673-149-9

Cover illustration by C. Michael Dudash
Cover designed by Brenda McGee

Unless otherwise referenced, scripture quotations are from: *The Holy Bible, New International Version* (NIV) © 1973, 1984 by International Bible Society, used by permission of Zondervan Publishing House

Printed in the United States of America

For information:
MULTNOMAH PUBLISHERS, INC.
POST OFFICE BOX 1720
SISTERS, OREGON 97759

Library of Congress Cataloging-in-Publication Data
Darty, Peggy.
    Promises/Peggy Darty.
        p.cm.   ISBN 1-57673-149-9 (alk. paper)   I. Title.
PS3554.A79P76   1997   97-26591
813'.54--dc21   CIP

97 98 99 00 01 02 03 — 10 9 8 7 6 5 4 3 2 1

For the Promise Keepers

*And especially for Julie,
who shared her story in the hope
that it would help other women.*

Guide me in your truth and teach me,
for you are God my Savior,
and my hope is in you all day long.

PSALM 25:5

Prologue

January 15, 1976

It was a cold winter day in north Georgia. The Coosa River, sluggish with ice, wound past a lonely-looking shack built on stilts for protection against the river's overflow. Eight-year-old Johnni Hankins huddled beneath the shack. Her mop of red hair fell away from her face as she tilted her head back, listening to the angry voice of a man inside the shack.

Suddenly, the door flew open. Julie, Johnni's twin, dashed onto the porch. A frail child with short brown hair, she too wore ragged jeans and a sweatshirt. She raced down the steps and headed toward the woods.

Tom Hankins exploded onto the porch. Fortyish, he was a large man with unkempt red hair and beard, wearing overalls and scuffed boots. He took off running after Julie.

"Julie, you'd better tell me where she is!" His gruff voice grated into the silence of the gray day.

Julie ran as fast as she could, arms pumping, feet flying. As she cast a glance over her shoulder, her face grimaced in terror. She had promised to take care of Johnni, her mischievous twin. *She had promised.* If her father found Johnni, he would beat her again. If only there were someone to help them…but there was no one. Bessie, her neighbor, spoke of a God, but Julie had only heard the word coming out of her father's mouth in vile curses.

"Stop running, Julie. *I mean it!*"

She stopped, grabbing the trunk of a tree, her breath jerking through her chest.

"Tell me where she is," he demanded. "She'll get a licking for sure this time."

Julie hesitated, her terror-stricken face turning away from the huge man before her. She knew the implications of his wrath, but she had to save Johnni.

Tears filled her eyes and trickled down her cheeks.

"Come on. I'll find her anyway."

She bit her lip until she tasted blood. Then the big hand reached down, gripping her arm.

"I said tell me!"

She began to sob, knowing it was useless. He would find out eventually. "Under the porch," she whispered, sinking into the mire of the swamp, her back pressed against a pine tree. She folded her arms over her knees, buried her head in her arms, and began to sob.

"There you are!" His bellowing voice rang through the woods as he thundered back to the porch.

Julie wanted to protect her sister, would have lied to protect her, but this time she was too frightened to lie. In telling the truth, she had broken her promise to Johnni. She thrust her fingers in her ears to shut out the sound of Johnni's scream.

CHAPTER

One

Friday, September 27, 1996

Oak Shadows Plantation sat on five hundred acres of towering oaks and stately pines. The plantation was located ten miles out of Springville, a sleepy little town that had once been the shipping point for the cotton kingdom that ruled Oak Shadows. But that was long ago. The cotton fields of Oak Shadows had been unfarmed for years; weeds, vines, and thick woods covered the ground.

A two-lane highway angled past other farms, once cotton plantations as well, to the boundaries of Oak Shadows. From the property line at the highway, the drive was unmarked, winding a quarter mile past woods, making one final, lazy curve before ending at the steps of the three-story mansion.

In spite of neglect, the house still held dominion over the land, like a brave yet aging mistress. It was a house that took one's breath away, despite its need of paint, for with the house came a hint of the glorious old South. This plantation had once been the talk of the county.

The house was white brick, layered with the dust of years

past. In late afternoon when the sunlight was soft, the rays gave a mellow glow to the house, and one could glimpse the beauty it had once been. Thick white columns and a long balcony braced the first and second floors. Smaller windows jutted out of the roof on the third floor. Behind the wide columns on the front, long windows flanked by dark green shutters were evenly spaced, with the same pattern repeated on the second floor. Side verandahs offered an extra touch of luxury, and the old Southern hospitality was still present in the oak rockers and a well-used swing on the lower verandah. A fanlight window arched above the front door, with narrow glass panels on each side of the door.

Inside, the house carried out the typical Southern floor plan: a hall sweeping past two front parlors, a dining room, and a kitchen. All the rooms were large and square, rising to high ceilings with crown moldings and rose medallions. From the front hall, a circular staircase wound upward to a spacious second story, and the third floor contained storage rooms that had not been used in a dozen or more years.

The right front parlor, once the sewing room for Confederate garments, was now an office furnished with a pleasant blend of old and new. Prized antique pieces were well placed among contemporary items, such as the desk where Elizabeth Calloway was seated, looking across at Julie Waterford, a petite woman with small features, brown hair, and brown eyes.

"This is quite a coincidence," Julie was saying. She spoke in a soft, shy voice. "I had no idea my new neighbor would be my psychologist, but this arrangement suits me perfectly. I developed agoraphobia a few months ago. I have to stay where I feel comfortable—my house and its surroundings. That's why I don't go into Atlanta anymore."

"Atlanta can be pretty intimidating." Elizabeth Calloway smiled gently. Elizabeth was five feet, six inches tall, with golden blonde hair, warm brown eyes, and a gentle smile that softened a square jawline.

"Atlanta is *very* intimidating for me now. That's why I appreciate living at the plantation." Julie shrugged. "Malcomb always referred to it as a farm, but to me it's still a plantation." She looked curiously at Elizabeth. "I was wondering—what brought you out here?"

"I was raised here at Oak Shadows," Elizabeth said, her eyes sweeping the room. "This place goes back five generations. The first O'Malley here was Irish, like so many others who settled in Georgia. Jack O'Malley came here with little money and big dreams of getting rich on cotton. Jack O'Malley was not afraid of hard work. Once he became successful, he built his wife's dream house. This house, which took years to complete, was finished the week before the war broke out.

"Naturally, Jack O'Malley became a Confederate soldier. There is even a wild rumor that his daughter, my great-great-grandmother, was a Confederate spy. Many of the O'Malleys are buried in the family cemetery on the grounds here, and some of the locals like to say that Jenny—that's the Confederate spy—" she explained, grinning, "strolls the grounds when the moon is full."

"What do you think?" Julie asked, wide-eyed.

"I don't believe in ghosts," Elizabeth answered quickly, "so the tale never bothers me." She hesitated, glancing up at an antique chandelier. "My parents were living in Marietta when I was born. Then my dad was killed in Vietnam when I was only four, and Mom and I moved back to Oak Shadows. I stayed until Mother and Grandmother decided I should attend a private boarding school in Atlanta, guaranteed to turn out debutantes. I'm afraid I broke their mold."

She laughed as she said the words, for it had long ceased to be a subject that bothered her. "During that time, Mother remarried an older man from Marietta, and they spend much of their time traveling. Mother wasn't interested in Oak Shadows after she married, and told Grandmother so. When Grandmother died last year, I inherited this place, and I've always loved it. So Katie and I came home."

She watched Julie's eyes drop to the simple gold wedding band on Elizabeth's left hand. Elizabeth sighed. "My husband stayed in Atlanta." She said nothing more. How could she explain the complicated separation that had torn their little family apart?

"I didn't mean to pry," Julie said in a rush, sinking deeper into the Queen Anne chair. She ran a small hand through her short brown hair, then adjusted the wire frame of her round glasses.

"You weren't prying," Elizabeth replied with a smile. "If there's an apology to be made, I owe it to you. I didn't mean to ramble so. I do feel it's important for you to know something about me if we're to work together."

She looked down at the open file on her desk, reading the notes she had taken on Julie. Julie's husband, Dr. Malcomb Waterford, had been killed in a car accident in the spring. "I'm sorry about your husband," she said, looking back at Julie. "He was a highly respected psychiatrist. I'm sorry I never met him. He bought the adjoining farm after I married and moved away."

Julie nodded, lowering her eyes. "Malcomb and I married two years ago; then we moved up here full-time last year. The past months have been extremely rough for me."

"And now you want to find your twin sister?"

"I want to stop her."

Elizabeth's eyes widened. "Stop her?"

"She's jealous of the way my life has turned out. By that, I mean I had good parents, a good education, and I married a man of status, although Malcomb was fifteen years older than I

16

and quite wealthy. Johnni's life——" She broke off as tears trembled in her eyes. "Johnni and I were eight years old when a social worker from Rome came to Woodfield and——" She swallowed hard, turning to stare through the window at the branches of the towering oaks that were starting to turn gold in the September light.

"You were placed in foster homes?" Elizabeth suggested, hoping to make the conversation easier for Julie.

Julie's eyes drifted back to Elizabeth. "I was adopted by a wonderful couple in Decatur, Philip and Sarah Harris. They've retired to Key West."

"I see."

"A few months after Malcomb died, I was taking a nap upstairs. The phone awakened me. Then I heard Johnni's voice. 'Julie,' she said, 'I've found you. And I've never forgiven you for ruining my life.'" Julie took a deep breath and looked at Elizabeth. "She truly hates me."

"Hates you?" Elizabeth repeated, unable to conceal her surprise. She lowered her eyes to the file, a method she often used when she needed to regain her composure. "Perhaps if you could just see Johnni face-to-face, rather than have these phone conversations——"

"I'm afraid to see her. Johnni was…is mean. There's no other word for it. Even as a child, she was always doing mean things, getting into trouble. The last time I saw her, I had been forced to tell on her. After that, a social worker came and…" Julie stopped, closing her eyes. "After the social worker came, our lives changed drastically."

She paused.

"Go on," Elizabeth prompted.

Julie didn't seem to want to go on; the past was obviously too painful for her to talk about now. Elizabeth made a note on the edge of the file to come back to this at a later date.

After a lengthy silence, Julie spoke again, her voice little more than a whisper. "During her last phone call, Johnni threatened me."

"Threatened you?" Elizabeth was puzzled. "How? What did she say?"

Julie took a deep breath and continued. "We have a birthday coming up two weeks from today. October 11. She said that something was going to happen…that there would be a terrible accident on or before our birthday.…" Julie's voice trembled as a sob rose in her throat. She stood, her hand gripping the back of the chair. "I'm not ready to talk about this. I really must go." She reached for her handbag.

Elizabeth pressed her hands against the desk and stood. "Would you mind if I asked Michael—my…husband—to look into this? He has a private detective agency, Searchers, that specializes in finding missing people. If he could find Johnni and the two of you could meet—"

Julie dabbed her eyes, staring at Elizabeth. "How would he find her? What would he do?"

Elizabeth considered the question. "Every case is different. He would want to talk with you about Johnni. He's very good, believe me. Perhaps you should take this threat seriously."

Their eyes locked. Neither wanted to refer to Malcomb Waterford's death, but the fact that a car accident had taken his life at the age of forty-three loomed foremost in Elizabeth's mind.

"I…don't know. Maybe someone could help," Julie replied dully, a look of torment replacing the tears.

"I want to help," Elizabeth responded gently. "While we work on finding Johnni, let me give you something to take home with you." She held out the book of Psalms to Julie. "I don't know if you're a believer, but if you'll just read a chapter now and then, I think you'll find strength and comfort in the verses."

"I know very little about the Bible," Julie said, staring at the book. "You really think this could help me?"

"Yes, I do. Just start with the Psalms, which are verses of comfort and thanksgiving. Then maybe I'll give you a complete Bible later on."

"Thanks," Julie reached out, slowly accepting the book of Psalms. "I'll see you next week."

She swept past Elizabeth and hurried out to her sleek gray Mercedes, which was parked in the driveway.

Elizabeth followed her to the door, staring after her. Julie Waterford was a woman on the brink of a nervous breakdown. Of that Elizabeth was certain. This sister, Johnni Hankins, had to be found. And the person who was best at finding people was her husband, Michael Calloway, whom she would be seeing very soon.

She sighed, closing the door. Hugging her arms against her chest, she thought of what she had said to Julie about Michael. He really was the best detective she had ever known. He worked hard, *too* hard. Their careers had always been in conflict. And yet she had always known that Michael was the best at his work. She and Michael had once joked that he searched for lost people, while Elizabeth searched for lost souls. Both were on different missions, yet, in some ways, their goals were the same.

She glanced down at her gold wristwatch. Soon it would be time to pick up Katie at school. Then Michael was coming after her around five this afternoon.

He avoided Oak Shadows—and Elizabeth herself—as much as possible. This weekend, however, Michael was taking Katie to a Braves game, and Katie had talked of nothing else at breakfast.

Tears stung Elizabeth's eyes. She should be going back to Atlanta with them. But their differences had evolved into conflicts she seemed unable to work through, at least for a while. It seemed she needed more time to sort things out. She closed her eyes and sighed. A month's separation had only made matters worse. How ironic that she, a Christian therapist, could give advice and comfort to others, yet she was unable to heal the rifts in her own marriage.

I did make an attempt to get help for us, she recalled. She had scheduled a meeting with their pastor. But the meeting had to be cancelled when a child was reported missing and Michael was called in on the case. Afterwards, she had neglected to reschedule. Was it because she was still seething over the fact that his work always came first? Or had she decided to dig her heels in and let Michael make the next move, just to see if he would?

Since he had done nothing, perhaps she should swallow her pride and suggest a marriage counselor. *But Michael would probably refuse, thinking I'd be trying to stack the deck.*

She had gone back and forth with him on so many things that she was exhausted. And she sensed that Michael was, too. But she had come to realize that marriage was always a work in progress, and they had both quit working.

Elizabeth wandered back to her desk and glanced down at the picture of rosy-cheeked Katie. Blonde curls framed an oval face with huge blue eyes and a warm smile guaranteed to melt the coldest heart. Katie was almost eight, the same age Julie had been when she had been adopted by the Harris couple. The mother had died, she assumed, or left the girls with their father, who must have been a brute of a man.

Elizabeth's life had not been without trauma, but she had always known she was loved. And she had the capacity to love. She still loved Michael; she still was committed to the promises she had made on their wedding day, even though they were living separately. Those marriage vows were sacred to her, and Michael claimed to feel the same way. Yet they couldn't seem to work their way through this terrible fog that enveloped them, driving them further and further apart.

Maybe she would speak with Michael about Johnni Hankins. Someone had to find her...and someone had to stop her from the torment she was causing Julie. She returned to her desk and sat down. Julie Waterford reminded her of a dainty little bird that had fallen from its nest and been stepped on by cruel people. She so wanted to help her, as she wanted to help the others who came to her with problems. This was the driving force that had sent her back to graduate school for her Ph.D.

Staring at Julie's file, Elizabeth thought of a colleague in Atlanta whom she had mentioned to Julie, a doctor who could offer her more help than Elizabeth. But when she'd mentioned him to Julie, she had refused. She wanted to work with Elizabeth, no one else. And she was not yet healed of agoraphobia. She had her groceries delivered, her mail was dropped at her mailbox, and a simple visit to Elizabeth's house seemed to throw her into a state of confusion.

Elizabeth got up from her desk and wandered to her well-stocked bookcase, pulling down a book that would deal with the symptoms and treatment of agoraphobia. She needed to review the book and think about how to help Julie. At least she would have something to occupy her weekend.

Laying the book on her desk, she hurried to get her car keys. Time to pick up Katie.

Twilight descended over Oak Shadows as Michael Calloway turned up the oak-lined driveway to the imposing mansion where Katie and Elizabeth now lived. He tried to calm the erratic beating of his heart as he pressed the accelerator, automatically hurrying to get the dreaded encounter with Elizabeth behind him.

21

Knowing Katie, she would be ready and waiting, and maybe he wouldn't even see Elizabeth. It would be so much easier for everyone if it worked out that way.

He parked in the driveway, trying not to think about how big the mansion was. Or how old. For the hundredth time, he tried to see the place through Elizabeth's eyes—an antebellum home that had reflected the grandeur of the county back in the 1800s, then had been refurbished again in the middle of this century. It was now time for another overhaul, one that would require more time and money than he and Elizabeth had. No, he caught himself, Elizabeth had the money, which put them back to square one—her family's money.

He stopped the car at the end of the drive and got out of his black Jeep, rotating his neck from right to left, trying to ease the tension that had been building there. He stretched his long legs as he made his way up the steps to the front door. He had not stopped all day, and even though he had spent the last half hour driving along, trying to relax, he felt even more tense than before.

Tall with broad shoulders and the muscular build of one who has spent years doing manual labor, he was a farm boy. He had spent his early years working on the farm, living in a modest little home with his parents and younger brother. They worked hard for every cent they earned.

He resembled his younger brother, Jay, only he looked a bit less rugged. Michael was slimmer, with more classic features, wide blue-gray eyes, and full lips. He wore his dark brown hair a bit longer than Jay, for he did not answer to the Atlanta Police Department, or anyone else, for that matter. He owned his own private agency, Searchers, Inc., but he and Jay were alike in their preference for investigating. They loved their work.

He raked through his thick brown hair, parting it on the side with his fingers in an unconscious habit. He had hurried home to change into jeans, a comfortable sport shirt, and his reliable Reeboks.

The sight of rocking chairs spaced about the verandah gave Michael a feeling of coming home. But this was not home, he reminded himself, glancing again at the peeling paint on the wide front columns. He had not yet found a permanent home, but his idea of one more closely resembled a simple, ranch-style house—like the one his parents owned just outside of Moonglow.

If only Elizabeth would give up this crazy dream, he thought with a sigh, squaring his shoulders and ringing the doorbell.

In seconds, the door cracked open.

"Oh, it's you," Elizabeth said, peering out at him.

"Yeah, with leprosy, bad breath, and flat feet."

"I meant," she said emphatically, "I'm not dressed yet, and I thought Mrs. Binkley had come early for me. Come in."

Reluctantly, Michael stepped inside, his eyes dropping in surprise to Elizabeth. She was wearing a terry-cloth housecoat, and her hair was rolled in electric curlers.

"Since you're taking Katie for the weekend," she explained quickly, "I volunteered to help Grace Binkley at the hospital in Marietta. Katie, your dad's here," she yelled up the stairs. "I'm ironing in the kitchen," she called over her shoulder to Michael.

Michael shoved his hands in his pockets and glanced up the circular stairway, wondering about Katie's room. He could hear the noises of Katie—the last-minute hurried bumps and slams as though she were running late today.

As he passed the adjoining parlors, he had a fleeting glimpse of the same faded brocade and damask in the long, high-ceilinged rooms he had seen on other visits. *Wonder what the heating bill would run*, he thought, sauntering on back to the kitchen where Elizabeth was putting up the ironing board.

His eyes roamed over the huge, older kitchen with pine cabinets and counters and the harvest gold appliances like those in his mom's kitchen. A yellow gingham tablecloth and matching ruffled curtains over the window gave the room a cozy touch. And the singing teakettle looked familiar. Without thinking, he walked over to turn off the kettle. Elizabeth had a habit of putting something on the stove, then forgetting it. It had been one of the jobs he automatically assumed after their marriage. His action brought another thought: It was quite possible she could accidentally burn this old relic down!

Elizabeth was casting a glance in his direction, but he said nothing about the red-hot eye of the stove. He was not going to fuss with her this time. But then he had no idea how a guy was supposed to carry on a casual conversation with his wife when they were living separately. He had never understood this "just friends" business that he heard about from divorced husbands when they spoke of their ex-wives. Even if they lived separately, he still wanted to be more than just friends; he wanted to be a family again. He just didn't know how to go about it.

He cleared his throat, attempting to start a reasonable conversation. "So what are you going to do at the hospital?" He tried to keep his tone casual, impersonal.

She grabbed a pair of black slacks from the kitchen chair and smoothed them onto the ironing board.

"I've offered to help out in the psychiatric unit. They're desperately in need of—"

"I thought you had your hands full here." *In this monstrosity*, he thought, glancing at the cracked ceiling in the kitchen.

"I do. But I want to learn more about mental illness. I can do that at the hospital, and maybe I can be of help."

She was frowning down at the slacks, as though uncomfortable with his presence. Or was it the conversation? Or both? He suddenly felt a line of tension strung between them, like an invisible wire growing more taut with each word they spoke to one another.

Feeling awkward and uncomfortable, he sauntered over to the kitchen sink, peering through the window to the backyard. Even in the growing darkness, he could see that the yard was badly in need of a lawn mower, and he was good at that…but he wasn't about to volunteer. Some mean spirit inside him wanted to prove to Elizabeth that she had taken on more than she could handle.

He glanced back at her. She had finished with the slacks and was positioning on the ironing board a pink crepe blouse, which she touched gently with the iron.

What she had said about the psycho unit bothered him. He didn't think it was a good idea, but he didn't know how to tactfully broach the subject.

He cleared his throat. "I, er, wouldn't have thought you'd want to work in a *psychiatric unit.*" He flinched inwardly at the way the words fell into sudden silence, like pebbles tossed into deep water. Although he had tried to conceal his distaste for the subject, he knew Elizabeth well enough to realize she had read his true meaning. Nevertheless, there was Katie to consider, and he didn't like the thought of her mother working in a psycho unit.

Elizabeth turned to face him, hands on hips. "Those people are human beings," she said coldly. For a moment, their stares locked; then she dropped her eyes to her blouse on the ironing board as she yanked up the iron again. "Michael, let's not argue."

Michael lifted an eyebrow, surprised by the sharpness of her tone. "I just made a simple statement. No need to get on the defensive."

Elizabeth avoided his eyes as she fumbled with the bow of the blouse. "Your attitude about my work always upsets me."

"I don't have an attitude." His voice had turned cold, but he couldn't seem to do anything about it.

"Really?" She glanced at him. "I could have sworn that's what started our problem last year."

"Problems. Plural."

"Michael, I don't have time," she snapped, dashing the iron up and down the sleeve of the blouse, not so carefully now.

Michael squared his shoulders, suddenly angry. "Wait a minute. Don't drop one of your little bombs, then run for cover. My attitude was—what's a good clinical term?—*healthy*. It was healthy about your going back to school the first time."

"Only the first time."

"I took my turn with dirty diapers and dirty dishes. And I worked to help you pay for that degree. You were an excellent first-grade teacher, Elizabeth."

Michael had begun to pace the floor. How had they dissolved into the old argument so easily, when all he wanted was to pick up Katie and leave?

Elizabeth was zigzagging the iron all over the blouse. "I tried to explain, but you refused to listen. My strength is in counseling, not teaching. I could reach those kids and their parents when—"

"There was plenty of time. I was working fourteen hours a day to build a business. I needed you."

Elizabeth stopped ironing and slammed the iron down, unaware that the collar was caught beneath the iron.

"No, you needed to control me. You resented it when my work became important."

"Like mine wasn't! Oh, I forgot. Being a private investigator wasn't cushy enough for the son-in-law of Mrs. R. J. Turner III."

Elizabeth gasped, horrified. "You leave my mother out of this."

"In all due respect to your mother, she wouldn't stay out of our lives. When she paid for your Ph.D., she was buying your freedom for you. That's what you want, isn't it?"

Tears filled Elizabeth's eyes, and Michael turned away, hating himself for the words that had tumbled hastily from his mouth. How had he forgotten every vow he had made to himself before leaving home? What had happened? Why couldn't he stop this bitterness that chewed at his insides night and day?

"I hate it when you two fight," Katie said quietly from the doorway.

Michael felt like a heel as he walked over and knelt down beside the daughter he adored. "We weren't fighting, honey. We were just having a little discussion."

"My blouse!" Elizabeth screamed from behind them.

Michael whirled. His eyes fell on the scorched blouse, and he felt more guilt well up within him. Why hadn't he kept his big mouth shut?

"Elizabeth, I'm sorry. I'll buy you another one. Come on, Katie, let's hit the road."

Katie dashed over to hug her mother; then they left in a rush.

As the front door banged behind them, Elizabeth stared at the ruined blouse. She picked it up and walked over to drop it into the trash can. Tears filled her eyes and spilled down her cheeks. What had happened to them? They had been a family and now…

She walked to the counter and grabbed a paper towel to wipe away her tears. In the process, her eyes drifted out the window to the distant woods, and for the first time she remembered Julie Waterford.

She hit her forehead with the palm of her hand. "I forgot to ask him," she wailed, making a dash to the front door. But his Jeep had already disappeared down the driveway.

She bit her lip. On Sunday she would talk to him about Julie Waterford. And she would be as professional as possible. They had to stop this bickering. It was terrible for all of them, especially Katie.

Two

Saturday, September 28

Julie studied the clothes in her closet, thinking of the lovely new fall line of clothes she had seen advertised in the newspaper. She desperately wished she could go into town, wander through the petite section of some of her favorite stores, and try on some outfits as she had once done. If she kept losing weight, she would be forced to order from one of those mail-order catalogs, as they had done as children once or twice a year. The rest of the time, she and Johnni obtained their clothing from the Salvation Army or Goodwill.

Shaking her short brown hair, she tried to push those thoughts from her mind before the headache started, the headache that always accompanied her memories of her early childhood.

She paced the bedroom, wondering if she dared venture from her space, her safe confines of home. But she knew she couldn't. Not without Malcomb. If he were alive, this awful agoraphobia would not have happened to her. And if he were alive, he would know how to handle Johnni.

Malcomb had been her anchor, the solid rock on which she

could lean, the binder that held her together, made her complete.

The book of Psalms that Elizabeth had given her was still there on the bedside table where she had left it the night before. She had read a few of the verses, and to her surprise, she had felt an odd comfort she could not explain. But then she had dozed off to sleep, and today she didn't feel like reading. A restlessness enveloped her. She wanted to get in her car, roll the windows down, feel the autumn breeze on her face as she drove someplace to shop. She thought of phoning her parents in Key West, but what could she say to them? They had been dear to come up and stay with her for a week after Malcomb's funeral. Then they had insisted that she return with them, but she had promised she would be fine. She had been relieved when they left, for all she wanted was to be left alone. If she called them now, they would again insist on her coming for an extended visit. And she had no desire to go to Key West. She wanted to stay here, in this place that she loved. And yet...

She wandered to her bedroom window and gazed out across the landscaped grounds. Walter had come yesterday to mow the lawn, trim the hedges, keep everything just as Malcomb had paid him to do for years. Sometimes she felt so isolated here, as though this were the only place in the world she could feel safe. Since Malcomb's death, it was all she could do to get out of bed each morning, go on with her day, do a bit of painting or walk around the familiar paths. How strange that a place she loved could at times, like today, become a prison to her.

Elizabeth was busily buying groceries and running errands in Marietta. There was a special bakery she particularly liked, and today she rushed through the door, breathing deeply of the bakery's rich yeasty aroma. Spotting the crowd, she realized that she was not the only one who had chosen to stop in on a Saturday morning to stock up on flavored teas and breads.

Joining the line waiting at the counter, she thought of the blueberry muffins Katie liked so well. And she thought of Michael. What were they doing on their special day together? As she thought of them and the fact that she was not with them, she suddenly didn't care about the breads or the teas. For one impulsive moment, she almost stepped out of line and left the bakery. But she would regret that decision later on in the week. She simply had to go on with her life, even though there was a huge hole in her heart without Michael.

Michael and Katie burst through the door of his town house, full of excitement over the Braves game they had just attended. Katie's cap was missing from her tumbled blonde curls, a mustache of mustard outlined her mouth, with another smear staining her jacket. Michael looked at her and chuckled.

"You gotta hit the tub, sweetie. Your mother would be upset with both of us if she could see you now."

"Daddy, we had a good time, didn't we?"

"Are you kidding? When Chipper Jones hit the winning home run, I've never heard such an uproar in Fulton Stadium. You know it's the last season of games in that stadium, hon. They're tearing it down to build a new one next year. That's why we gotta win the series!"

Katie turned to stare up at her father. In her eyes, he was the most wonderful man in the world. His face was dominated by deep blue-gray eyes, and she imagined he must be very handsome to women. She had noticed a few women staring at him at the ballpark. She never thought about his looks; to her, he was just her dad, and she loved him with all of her heart. She just didn't understand why he and Mom couldn't solve their problems. She knew her mom still loved him from the way she looked at his picture in her room. So what was the big deal?

She sighed heavily, tugging off her jacket. "Dad, I wish you still lived with us."

The happy expression that Michael had worn since Glavin struck out the first batter now faded from his face. A dark frown ridged his forehead as he tilted his head to the side and looked sympathetically at his daughter.

"Hey, you and I still have fun, don't we?"

Katie's blue eyes turned pensive. "Yeah, but…" Her voice trailed off as the blue eyes, which were so like her father's eyes, drifted into space. She was thoughtful for a moment as Michael searched for the right thing to say.

"Well, we're learning a lot about life together, pal. Now… off to the tub and your pajamas. Then I have a new book to read you at bedtime."

"A new book? Great!" She dashed up the stairs to the bath.

Michael still lived in the town house he had shared with Elizabeth for the past six years. Before that, they had lived in a one-bedroom apartment, with Katie's little crib tucked in a corner nearby. Maybe every woman wanted a big house, was that it? Was that what had pulled Elizabeth out to Oak Shadows, that sprawling old relic filled with ghosts, according to local legend? Neither he nor Elizabeth believed in ghosts; still, he couldn't help wondering how Katie felt when the gruesome subject was mentioned.

He heard the water running in the tub, and his mind switched back to the words she had spoken earlier.

"Dad, I wish you still lived with us."

He should have come right out and said it: *Your mother and I are both too stubborn for each other, Katie.* But he had kept silent. It seemed childish and downright embarrassing for two adults to be locked in an emotional tug-of-war, particularly when Katie was on the losing end of the rope. He kicked back in his recliner, thinking. How could he run a thriving detective agency when he lived an hour away, up at Oak Shadows? He supposed he could hop into the car at two in the morning and head into town when a distress call came in. Or they could spend their weekends at Oak Shadows, as Elizabeth had first suggested to him. But he had balked at that. Okay, so he was stubborn.

This was hard, really hard. "God, help us," he said quietly, closing his eyes and leaning his head against the back of the chair.

Johnni sat before the mirror, studying the makeup she had so carefully applied. The ivory foundation was a smooth sheen over her pale face, and the second coat of mascara had worked its magic on wide emerald eyes. She lifted a polished nail to flick a strand of red hair back from her face, wondering about the hairstyle. The thick strands, styled in a short shag, suited her. For a while, at least. A blank stare met her as she gazed at the face in the mirror, feeling a mixture of love and hate for the woman who stared back at her.

Studying the mirror image, she felt a thrill of pleasure at the diamond earrings glinting softly in her ears. She tilted her head slightly, enjoying the sparkle in the soft glow of the lamp. Her eyes moved down to the low-cut black blouse. It was silk, imported, something from Sak's that Johnni Hankins could not afford. But she loved wearing it. The silk caressed her skin, intoxicating her with a sense of luxury. It was going to be a wonderful night.

Slowly, her eyes dropped to her hands, folded on the dressing table, grasping a wad of hundred-dollar bills. Shopping, dinner at an exclusive restaurant, and perhaps tonight she would find a man to fill the lonely void within, to quiet the voices that whispered to her.

She tilted her head back and studied the purple lipstick as her mouth widened in a pleased smile. She felt wonderful.

Three

Sunday, September 29

Michael and Katie drove toward Moonglow, with Katie chattering excitedly in her usual fashion. She loved life; she especially loved talking about everything she observed or thought or heard.

"I haven't seen Granny and Grandpa in weeks. Do you think Granny will have a lot of good things to eat today?" she asked.

Michael grinned. "Your grandmother always has good things to eat! With today being Sunday, you can expect that dining-room table to be filled. However, as our contribution, I think I'll stop and pick up some barbecue at Smoky's. Granny and Grandpa don't get over to Smoky's very often, and they love his barbecue. What do you think? Is that a good idea?"

"Yeah." She grinned.

Michael was turning into the drive that circled the concrete-block building, seeking a parking space among the variety of vehicles.

"Dad, look at the smoke!" Katie pointed.

"Yep, that's Smoky's outdoor grill. That's hickory smoke; it makes a good fire for barbecuing."

"Are we gonna eat something here?" Katie glanced from the grill back to her father.

"Well," Michael said, "we don't want to hurt Grandma's feelings by filling up before we even get to her house. Maybe just a taste or two wouldn't hurt, if you can keep a secret." Michael grinned across at her, knowing how she loved secrets.

"I won't tell," she solemnly promised.

Michael got out of his Jeep and came around to open Katie's door. They had long ago made a deal that she never hop out of the Jeep on her own, without her father right beside her. She was spontaneous and impulsive, which worried Michael. He constantly warned her about jumping out of the Jeep and into the path of an oncoming vehicle, which was why he always insisted that he open the door for her.

With her hand in his, they sauntered toward the barbecue pit, where Smoky was hard at work, spooning his famous sauce over several slabs of ribs. He wore his usual chef's apron, decorated with a few traces of red sauce.

"Hey, Smoky!" Michael called to him.

Smoky looked up quickly, and his white chef's cap inched back a bit on his round head.

"Michael Calloway! How you doin', buddy? And who is this little beauty with you?"

Katie giggled.

"This is my daughter, Katie. Katie, say hello to the best chef in Georgia."

"Hello," she said, flashing him a charming grin.

"She's a doll, Michael. Didn't take after you, thank goodness!"

"Right. She looks like her mother," Michael agreed. "Think we could pick up a slab of ribs to go?"

"Sure can. I'm cooking plenty today, with it being Sunday. How's Jay, by the way?"

"He and Tracy are like two lovebirds in a nest. Couldn't be happier."

Smoky chuckled. "Glad to hear it. Everybody's still talking about how they cracked the DeRidder case." His smile faded. "That was a sad situation."

"Yeah. Hey, are you staying busy?" he asked quickly, not wanting to linger on the subject of marriage. Nobody in Moonglow knew that he and Elizabeth were separated. His parents certainly didn't, and he wanted to be the first to break the bad news.

"Yeah, I'm always busy," Smoky answered. "But me and the wife are taking some time off to drive up to the Smokies in a couple of weeks. The trees should be in perfect color by then."

"Have a good trip." Michael patted him on the shoulder. "You've earned it."

"Tell them inside I said to give you the biggest slab of ribs in the kitchen," Smoky called to him as they turned for the door.

"Thanks." Michael grinned. "Good to see you again, Smoky."

"You too. Tell your old man I said hi."

Michael nodded and steered Katie inside the crowded restaurant. There were few people Michael knew here nowadays, but he waved at one or two friendly faces. He had been gone from Moonglow for over ten years, and some of the kids he remembered last seeing on bicycles and skates now drove pickup trucks. He shook his head. Where had the years gone?

"Dad, I don't see anything I would rather have than Grandma's chocolate cake," Katie said, eyeing the display of pies.

"Me either. Let's just wait."

As they left with their order, Katie linked her arm through his and looked up at him, suddenly troubled.

"What if Grandma doesn't have any chocolate cake?" she worried.

He put her in the Jeep, set the wrapped ribs on the back floorboard, then paused to wink at his daughter. "Knowing that we're coming, I can almost guarantee that your grandmother will have some of her famous chocolate cake."

Katie giggled with delight.

The sound of her laughter was like music to his ears as Michael got in the Jeep, and they drove up the quiet valley, shaped like a crescent moon. The area was situated on the high banks of Rabun Creek in northeast Georgia's Rabun County. He loved coming back here, but he couldn't imagine living here again.

Unlike Elizabeth, who was so eager to go back to her roots.

At the thought of his troubled marriage, all the joy he had been feeling began to fade. He had tried to keep the news of his separation a secret from his parents, but there was no way he could keep it secret any longer. And he didn't want to set the wrong example for Katie by misrepresenting the facts or out-right lying. He would simply tell them the truth, but it wasn't going to be easy....

Ellie and Mike Calloway were seated on the front porch, watching the drive. Both leaped to their feet at the sound of Michael's vehicle.

As soon as he had stopped the Jeep, Mike was at his side, Ellie on the passenger's side, opening the door for Katie. Everyone was talking at once, hugging and laughing. Then suddenly there was a gap in conversation as Ellie looked first at Mike, then at Michael.

"Elizabeth couldn't make it?" she asked tactfully.

"No, she couldn't," Michael replied, hoping they wouldn't have to get into the subject until later.

"Grandma, did you make chocolate cake?" Katie asked, saving all of them a moment's embarrassment.

"Now just what makes you think I would do that?" Ellie

laughed, hugging her granddaughter.

Ellie was a tall, large-framed woman, a well-suited match for her husband, tall and husky and a bit loud. Yet Ellie's calming nature had a way of keeping her husband soothed down.

"She better have made us cake. Right, Katie?" Michael said.

"Right!"

Everyone was laughing again, and Michael was relieved that the subject of Elizabeth had been stalled for a while longer.

After church when Elizabeth returned home alone to the huge empty house, a lump the size of a rock clogged her throat, and tears rushed to her eyes. She unlocked the door and walked into the long hall, dropping her car keys into the dish on the marble washstand.

"You are not going to feel sorry for yourself," she said into the stillness of the house.

Sunday. Alone. The high heels she hated to wear seemed to echo throughout the entire house as she crossed the hardwood floors and climbed the stairs to her bedroom, eager to get out of her Sunday dress and into something comfortable.

Every sound haunted her, for it reminded her of how alone she felt without Katie. Without Michael. What was she doing here all by herself? Had she made the biggest mistake of her life, trying to restore Oak Shadows? There was so much restoration to be done that the details alone were mind-boggling, not to mention the time and the expense.

She walked along the upstairs corridor to her bedroom, trying to find a ray of encouragement from the excellent sermon she had just heard. It had to do with sowing good seeds and reaping a harvest of joy in return. While she had applied that parallel to her life, specifically her family and her torn marriage, another thought popped into her mind as she entered the bedroom.

Gripping the spindle post of the cherrywood bed, she reached down to yank her heels off while her thoughts drifted to Grandmother's garden, which had been neglected for years while Grandmother was bedridden. Throughout her years at Oak Shadows, there had been a cook and a housekeeper and a lawn service, but her grandmother had insisted on tending the garden herself. Apparently, working in her flower beds had provided therapy for this strong, kind woman. She loved to plant her seedlings in the earth and imagine the rainbow of flowers that would burst through the soil in the spring. And the lovely little flowers always came up, to everyone's delight. Her grandmother had been very good at choosing the seeds, tending the soil, nourishing the baby flowers.

Changing into comfortable baggy pants and a loose T-shirt, Elizabeth felt a rush of nostalgia as she recalled her grandmother in her sundress and the wide-brimmed hat that shielded her delicate pink skin. She had been such a nurturing woman in all that she did.

She put on socks and tennis shoes and raced back down the stairs, pausing in the kitchen for a microwave dinner and iced tea. As she waited for the buzzer on the microwave to signal that lunch was ready, she stared through the window to the expansive backyard. The pretty flower garden, Grandmother's pride and joy, was now consumed with weeds and debris. Elizabeth felt sad remembering how her grandmother had so painstakingly tended that garden.

Elizabeth had an idea, and with it came a surge of hope. Here was something she could start on right away. She could spend her idle hours restoring the family garden, and this would bring her great pride. She didn't know if she had a green thumb, but she did enjoy plants and flowers. And she had loved tagging after her grandmother in the garden, using the tiny spade and gloves her grandmother had bought for her as they worked side by side. Her grandmother had been so patient with her, and in her memory, that gentle voice still echoed in her ears, as her grandmother spoke of planting, nurturing, loving....

She hurried through her lunch, remembering that a discount store in Springville would be open on Sunday afternoon. The store had a small area devoted to gardening supplies. What fun it would be to spend her lonely afternoon buying seedlings, ground cover, a spade, and gloves. It could be a wonderful project for her, one in which she could involve Katie. The tradition that her grandmother had begun would continue. Katie would love it.

Four

L ate that afternoon, the distant sound of a car engine pene-
trated Elizabeth's thoughts as she knelt in the old garden,
yanking weeds from the ground while mentally outlining
her flower garden. The sound grew closer and she stood, dust-
ing her pants and slapping the dirt from her gloves. She was so
thirsty she could hardly swallow, and she looked a mess, but
she felt better than she had in days.

So many good memories had drifted through her mind during the afternoon, memories of her life here at Oak Shadows.
Deep in her heart, she felt she was doing the right thing, coming home, trying to restore Oak Shadows.

Walking quickly around the side of the house, she expected
to see Michael dropping Katie off, and she had decided to invite
him to stay for iced tea. She had to swallow her pride and discuss Julie Waterford with him.

As she hurried around the corner of the house, she came up
short. To her surprise, it was not Michael but rather Ellie
Calloway getting out of the car, while Katie came running up
the front sidewalk.

Elizabeth called out to them and waved as they approached.

She glanced first at the happy face of her daughter, then to her mother-in-law, whom she dearly loved.

"Ellie," she said as she reached her side, "I'm such a mess that I can't hug you, but I'm delighted to see you."

Ellie smiled, deepening the laugh lines around her friendly hazel eyes. "I'm used to dirt, honey. I'd rather have a hug." As the two women embraced, memories flooded through Elizabeth's mind: Saturday fish fries, complete with Ellie's special hush puppies, wonderful Sunday meals, long talks over coffee. Suddenly, tears filled her eyes, and before she could lower her lashes, Ellie had seen them and merely squeezed her hand in quiet understanding.

"We've had a good day," Ellie said casually, as though bringing Katie here, rather than Atlanta, was nothing out of the ordinary for her.

Elizabeth smiled at Katie's little back as she hurried toward the front door.

"Mom, I have to call Brooke," she called over her shoulder.

"Okay." She turned back to Ellie. "Brooke is her new best friend. Ellie, do you have time for a glass of tea? I'm dying of thirst. As you can see, I've been working in Grandmother's flower garden all afternoon."

"I'd love a quick glass of tea, but then I have to head back. Revival services are starting this evening at our church, and I'm one of the hostesses for refreshments afterwards."

Elizabeth did a quick mental tally of the amount of time it had taken her to make the drive from Moonglow and felt a twinge of irritation at Michael for imposing on his mother.

She patted Ellie's arm. "Then let's hurry." Elizabeth led the way up the steps, catching up with Katie in the hall. "Missed you, hon." Elizabeth reached down to give her a hug.

"Yuk," Katie said, drawing back from Elizabeth. "You're all dirty."

She laughed. "When did a little dirt ever bother you, prissy?"

Katie giggled, grabbing the banister.

"This really is a lovely place, Elizabeth," Ellie said. Her hazel eyes roamed over the faded wallpaper, the crown moldings, lingering on the massive chandelier. Elizabeth glanced at her mother-in-law, thinking only Ellie could be so generous, so understanding.

"I have to hurry and call Brooke," Katie yelled, dashing up the stairs.

Elizabeth was glad she and Ellie would have a few moments of privacy. What might have been an awkward situation would probably be averted by the grace Ellie possessed. She was too considerate to ask questions. She had never pried. This time, however, Elizabeth felt the need to do some explaining as soon as they sat down for tea.

In the meantime, she noticed Ellie's curious expression as she looked from room to room.

"I'll give you a quick tour," Elizabeth offered. "There's the front parlor—" she pointed to the left—"with its matching parlor on the right. I'm using that one as an office. Behind the parlor on the left is the dining room, and behind that the kitchen. And our *tea*," she emphasized.

She led the way into the kitchen and washed her hands while Ellie settled herself at the kitchen table, looking over the tall white cabinets, lingering on the glass-paneled ones that displayed a collection of teapots. Elizabeth dried her hands on a cup towel, retrieved two tall glasses from the cabinets, and began to fill them with ice.

"This must have been a wonderful place to grow up," Ellie said, absorbing the spaciousness that was missing from her own small home.

"Yes, it was," Elizabeth said with a sigh as she removed a large pitcher from the refrigerator and poured tea. She took a seat opposite Ellie and smiled gently. "But remember I grew up without a father. Michael was *so* blessed to have two wonderful parents."

Their eyes met over the glasses. Ellie asked no questions; she merely gave a warm smile to Elizabeth, and again Elizabeth thought how fortunate she was to have Ellie for her mother-in-law.

"Ellie, as always, you're too gracious to say anything, but I want you to know that I still love Michael, and I pray we can work things out. It's very complicated, or maybe we're both just being a bit stubborn."

Ellie bit her lip, her eyes filling with tears.

"Oh, Ellie." Elizabeth reached across the table, squeezing her hand. "I wouldn't hurt you for anything in the world. And I don't want to hurt Michael. But we have some biggies to work through." She dropped her eyes. "We're both too committed to our work, you know that. As for why I'm here..." She hesitated, searching for the right words. "It's hard to explain to anyone, but ever since Grandmother died, I feel as though I have a magnet attached to my heart that connects back to the front door of this house. You see, I'm the last of the original O'Malley clan. I feel such a responsibility toward this place. I...I can't explain it, but I'm just drawn back here in a way that..." She broke off, again searching for words. "Michael calls it an obsession, and I know it doesn't make sense to anyone."

Ellie said nothing; she merely squeezed Elizabeth's hand, trying to understand.

Elizabeth looked at Ellie. "One of the things I've always admired about you is that you never, ever gave an opinion about anything your sons and their wives did, unless asked. Then you had this tactful way of saying, 'Well, since you've asked, I'll tell you what *I* would do.'"

They were both smiling through their tears.

"I know if I ask you," Elizabeth continued, feeling sick at heart, "you would say my place is with my husband. And that would be the right thing to say. But—" she drew a deep breath as her eyes trailed over the kitchen of her childhood—"I can't convey to anyone how important this is to me."

Ellie had reached into her handbag for a Kleenex and was dabbing at her eyes. "The grandmother you loved so much has passed away, and your mother has remarried and is in Europe. This wonderful place is important to you because it's your heritage. I can understand that sense of wanting to come home, even though I've never left Moonglow. I'm not going to give any opinions, Elizabeth, because I'm not walking in your shoes, or Michael's either. But I am going to pray for both of you. God can work this out for you two, as long as you remain faithful to him. And I know that both of you are committed to your marriage vows. Let me assure you of one thing: Michael still loves you as much as ever. All I have to do is look in his eyes to see it."

Elizabeth fell silent, unable to speak around the lump stuck in her throat.

"Well, I really do have to go," Ellie sighed, "even though I don't want to leave. But I've promised to be back for tonight."

Elizabeth nodded. "I understand, and you were very sweet to take the time to drive Katie over here. Please come back when you can stay longer."

Ellie nodded as she finished her tea and stood. "I will. Love you," she said, giving her a quick hug before hurrying out of the kitchen. "Bye, Katie," she called up the stairs.

"No doubt she's deep in conversation with Brooke," Elizabeth said apologetically as she followed Ellie to the door. "I hope she's thanked you for a good time."

"She did. She and Michael just came for the day, but we enjoyed every minute. She's making friends at her new school, she told me."

47

Elizabeth nodded. "Especially with Brooke. They bonded right away. Brooke's family is great, and they only live a mile from here. Brooke is a very sweet kid. I'm glad they're friends."

"Good." Ellie walked through the door with Elizabeth lingering behind. For a moment Ellie paused on the front steps, inhaling deeply and glancing at the towering oaks. She looked back at Elizabeth. "I can see why you love this place." She gave her a quick smile before hurrying back to the car.

Unable to watch her leave, Elizabeth walked back to the kitchen, feeling an almost unbearable pain in her heart. Katie had wonderful grandparents and a loving father. She was a fortunate little girl.

The smell of dirt from the garden was strong in her nostrils, and she allowed her eyes to trail down her dirty T-shirt and slacks. She didn't know when she had looked so grimy, but she was deriving real satisfaction from restoring her grandmother's garden. With every weed that she pulled, it was as though she were yanking out bad seed, trying to restore the earth to its former beauty.

In a way, that's what she did in her job, as well. She wanted to help people weed the misery and confusion from their lives, restore hope and joy, rediscover happiness once again.

Her eyes strayed toward the kitchen window as she remembered her neighbor, Julie Waterford, and the upheaval and confusion in her life. She must speak to Michael about Johnni Hankins. He could find her; she had faith in him. Elizabeth felt one of the keys to Julie's problems lay in Johnni's hands. Finding Johnni would start the healing process for Julie. Or so she hoped.

Five

Monday, September 30

Michael stepped off the elevator, the newspaper inches from his face as he walked down the corridor past several offices, pausing at the wooden door with *SEARCHERS* black-lettered across the center of the door. Scanning the sports section, he fumbled for the knob, opened the door, and entered his office.

"The coffee is made."

He closed the paper and smiled across at Anita Jackson, a tall woman in her fifties with salt-and-pepper hair, a few wrinkles bracketing her eyes and mouth, and a pair of soft brown eyes set in a round face. She was the model of efficiency, and Michael continually counted her among his blessings. She was organized, intuitive, dependable, and knew exactly how he liked his coffee. Furthermore, she wasn't above delivering a mug of coffee to his desk.

"Have I told you lately that I appreciate your hard work?" He gave Anita a big smile and a wink.

She nodded. "Yes, but I always like hearing it. You've had half a dozen calls already."

Michael sighed, glancing around his neat office. The reception area was small, with a plaid sofa and matching chairs placed opposite a coffee table stacked with magazines, all arranged by Anita's perfect hand.

He headed for his office, thinking of the day ahead. The room was large and conservatively decorated in greens and browns. A mahogany desk and swivel chair dominated the room with a Queen Anne chair positioned opposite the desk. The walls held wildlife prints along with an autographed picture of the Atlanta Braves. It was home for him, the only place that was not a tomb of loneliness since Elizabeth and Katie moved out a month ago.

The thought pierced his heart like a spear as he recalled Sunday and the tears his mother had shed upon learning that he and Elizabeth were living apart.

"You two made a promise the day you spoke your wedding vows," she reminded him.

"I know, and neither of us wants a divorce. But just let us work this out on our own," he pleaded quietly. With the wisdom typical of his mother, she dropped the subject and went in search of her granddaughter, who was perched on her grandfather's knee, listening to the latest fishing tale.

"Ready to make chocolate chip cookies, Katie?" she inquired. Later, she offered to drive Katie back to Elizabeth at Oak Shadows, sparing Michael the pain.

Michael removed his navy blazer and hung it in the closet beside the door as Anita entered with a steaming mug of coffee.

"You look nice this morning," she observed, looking him over. She persisted in saying that, according to her age, she could be his mother. He doubted that. Still, she looked after him with much the same care. Her eyes swept down his pinstriped red-and-white shirt to the navy slacks. Michael knew she was patrolling for loose threads, missing buttons, a dry-cleaning tag.

"Glad I pass inspection," he teased, gratefully accepting the coffee. "Did I tell you I'm placing a star on our church tree this year in your honor?"

"You did, and I'm touched. Now about those calls—"

He put up a hand. "I'll return every one of them. But I gotta tell you, Anita, I'm tired of finding husbands who don't want to be found."

"What about children who *want* to be found? The mayor still brags about your finding his son. Oh, and Bill Peterson at Mental Health called. Said he's in the Rotary Club with you and that you volunteered to employ a mentally challenged person. They have one. His name is Edwin, and he can do office work."

"Good. Call back and tell them we'll take Edwin."

"Okay. We can use some help with the wastebaskets and—

"No," Michael interrupted. "The janitor does that. I want to boost his self-esteem."

"You're right." Anita smiled. "And that's very sensitive of you." She made a note, then glanced down at the stack of phone slips. She retrieved one and waved it before his face. "You might want to return this call first."

It was Elizabeth at home. Since he dealt with danger on a daily basis, his first thought was of Katie, but Anita was quick to reassure him.

"Everything is fine. She just wants to talk with you about one of her clients."

"One of her clients?" he echoed coolly. "When has she ever consulted me about her work?" For that matter, why did she even want to talk with him, after their scene in the kitchen on Friday evening?

"Come on, Michael," Anita scolded gently. "It's the pot calling the kettle black when you complain of her being too devoted to her work."

"I never said that," he answered carefully, aware he was already on the defensive. As Anita's eyes lingered on him, he reached for the phone. Then Anita hurried out of the office, tactfully closing the door behind her. His hand punched the numbers on the keypad as he cradled the phone against his cheek and thought of Elizabeth.

When she answered, the sound of her voice still brought a rush of emotion to him, but he tried to push aside his feelings.

"Hi. Anita said you wanted me to call you," he stated coolly. "What's up?"

There was a moment's pause, and he wondered how she felt when they tried to have an objective conversation in view of all that had happened.

"Katie and I are fine," she answered slowly. "She had a great time over the weekend. And it was good to see your mother again."

Michael released the breath he had been holding. He was tempted to apologize again about the blouse. *Better avoid the subject*, he decided.

"I'm calling about one of my clients," she rushed on, the breathless quality of her voice a signal to Michael that she wanted to avoid their personal lives.

"Oh?" he asked, puzzled. He fumbled with his coffee mug, curiosity mounting as he waited for her reply.

"I'm dealing with a very troubled woman—my neighbor, actually—who is desperate to find her twin sister. The sister, Johnni Hankins, is apparently psychotic. She calls Julie, making terrible threats. Julie has Caller ID, but Johnni always places her calls from pay phones. Or she blocks the calls. 'Unavailable' always comes up on her Caller ID."

Absently, Michael reached for a pad. "You must be concerned for your client if you're calling me about her. What exactly do you want me to do?"

There was a momentary pause. "I want you to locate Johnni for us. Julie Waterford lost her husband this past year, and that was tough enough. Now this twin sister, who, by the way, was separated from Julie at the age of eight, is insanely jealous because Julie has wealth and status. Apparently Johnni has had nothing but poverty and problems. I know it doesn't make sense, but I'm afraid if this twin isn't stopped, Julie is going to have a breakdown. She's very close now. And this sister has threatened her with some kind of 'accident' before their next birthday, which happens to be a week from Friday—October 11."

There was a momentary pause on the other end of the wire as Michael listened to Elizabeth's deep sigh. "You're the best at finding people, Michael, even *I* have to admit that."

"That's quite a compliment, coming from you." He heard the touch of sarcasm in his voice and bit his lip.

"Michael, let's not argue anymore. Katie doesn't need it."

He sighed heavily. "Neither do we."

"I agree." There was a moment's hesitation. "Julie is capable of paying whatever is necessary to find her sister."

"Okay. I'll connect you back to Anita. Tell her to give you the first appointment."

"The problem is," she said gently, "this woman has agoraphobia. Fear of spaces outside her own environment. She doesn't go into Atlanta anymore."

"Agoraphobia," he repeated, shaking his head. "I've never known anyone with that condition. What do you do to help her?"

"It's a slow process. I'll explain it when there's more time."

Michael's respect for her work swelled. Elizabeth was highly intelligent; he had always known that. He began to imagine the combination of her gentle voice and sharp mind working together to help people.

"Okay. Where does she live?"

"She owns the farm adjoining mine...."

The farm adjoining mine. Those words lunged at Michael like a pit bull going for his ankle. Ever since Elizabeth had inherited Oak Shadows, there had been nothing but problems. Now she had the audacity to ask him to go to her neighbor's farm, when he hated the thought of being within a mile of Oak Shadows.

Now it was his turn to heave a deep sigh.

"Michael, this woman is on the brink of a breakdown. You could help her." The voice was soft and persuasive, sending a jolt all the way to his toes. He closed his eyes, pressing the receiver tighter against his cheek. He couldn't say no to her, he knew that. But then again, he couldn't just cave in the first time she called. He decided to try and strike a happy medium.

"I'll have Anita make an appointment with—what is her name?"

"Mrs. Malcomb Waterford. Her husband was a highly respected psychiatrist who taught at Emory."

He nodded. "I've heard of him. I'll see what I can do."

"Thanks, Michael." Her voice softened, and the ache in his heart intensified.

"You're welcome," he answered. "And by the way, you have a neat daughter."

"Maybe she's a bit like her father."

He sat up straighter, pleased by the compliment.

"Gotta go," she said suddenly, as though needing to back-track, erase the compliment, stifle all hope of reconciliation.

"See—talk to you later," he amended.

Before he could reflect further, Anita was at the door, announcing the arrival of his first appointment for the day. He was glad. He didn't want to think about Elizabeth.

"While I'm returning calls and seeing this client, will you please see if you can set me up an appointment with Mrs.

Malcomb Waterford today? Ask her if I can see her sometime after twelve." He hesitated. "The woman is sick, so I'll drive up there," he said hastily. "Tell her Elizabeth asked me to do that."

Anita smiled warmly. "Of course."

He grinned, knowing how much Anita liked Elizabeth.

Six

———————

Michael slowed at the driveway that ran beside a small wooden sign lettered *WATERFORD FARM*. He guided his black Jeep up the long driveway canopied with beautiful oaks and past a well-landscaped lawn to a red-brick mansion, parking in front of the crescent marble steps.

"Hello, Tara," he sighed, looking over the brick mansion. He could never feel at home in a place like this. He tried not to think of Oak Shadows.

His eyes traced the thick white columns of the elegant house before him. He just didn't fit in places like this, not Michael Calloway, a farm boy from rural Moonglow. Well, he was here. Might as well go on with the plan.

He got out of his Jeep and climbed the concrete steps, glancing absently at a miniature marble statue on the front porch. He rang the doorbell and waited, thinking about what Elizabeth had told him about Julie Waterford.

The door opened and a tiny woman with short brown hair peered at him through glasses that seemed to magnify the depths of her brown eyes. She was dressed in a white silk blouse and black slacks and was cradling a white Persian.

"Hi. I'm Michael Calloway." He nodded at her and glanced again at the cat, thinking of a kitten he had once rescued for Katie.

"I'm Julie Waterford," the woman answered in a soft shy voice. "Want to come in?"

Michael stepped over the threshold into a marble-tiled foyer with a broad circular staircase that seemed to float upward to the second and third floors. His eyes dropped back to the foyer, to an abstract painting on the wall.

"That is not my best work," Julie said, following Michael's eyes to the painting.

"You're an artist?" Michael inquired, looking at the smudges of color that made no sense to him.

"I try to be an artist. Come this way." There was a breathless, little-girl quality to her voice. He was somewhat curious about her shy nature; after all, she had been married to a prominent psychiatrist and lived in a fabulous home. Where was the self-confidence?

Michael followed her into a large den with oak paneling, overstuffed sofas, and chairs. In the far end of the room, a stone fireplace was flanked by bookshelves lined with volumes of books. A black Persian leaped from the arm of a chair, arching his back at Michael.

"Out of the way, Lucifer," Julie scolded softly, then glanced over her shoulder at Michael. "He's the mischievous one. Angel here is a love." She smiled at the Persian she still cradled in her arms as she took a seat on a multi-plaid sofa.

It was a very pretty white cat, Michael noted, thinking how Katie would adore it. A hiss and scampering feet pulled his attention back to Lucifer, who was scowling back at Michael. The black Persian obviously considered Michael an unwelcome guest in Lucifer's domain as he skulked out the door.

"Won't you have a seat?" Julie asked.

Michael settled into the most comfortable looking chair—a butter-soft recliner—which he imagined had been Dr. Waterford's favorite. He could smell something nice in the air—something that took him back to his childhood. Fried chicken!

This woman must have a cook and a maid and all the trimmings.

Michael's eyes swept the room, lingering on the oil painting of a middle-aged man with a thin face, keen blue eyes, and receding brown hair. "That's Dr. Waterford, I assume?"

"Yes." Julie smiled sadly at the painting.

Michael nodded. He remembered reading about the prominent psychiatrist who had died in a car accident.

"He was a brilliant man," Julie continued. "I met him at Emory when I was a student." She hesitated, turning her eyes from the portrait to Michael. "Unlike his first wife, I didn't resent the time he spent with his work."

Michael nodded. "That sounds familiar." The words came out before he could stop them, for it was an admission more to himself than to Julie.

"What do you mean?" she asked, tilting her small head to study him thoughtfully.

Michael sighed. "I resented Elizabeth's ambition at first. I'm coming to realize she worked hard to complete her education."

"And you're still in love with her," she concluded.

He took a deep breath. "Could we get back to my reason for driving out here?"

Julie gave him a knowing smile. "You're a swan."

"I beg your pardon?" He stared at her.

"A swan mates for life."

"Hey, do I look like a swan?" he teased, then shook his head. How had they gotten so far off the track? "Er, Mrs. Waterford—"

"Just call me Julie."

"And I'm Michael. Elizabeth tells me you need to find your sister," he said, trying to get right to the point.

Julie looked startled for a moment, then began to stroke her cat, staring at its soft white fur. "My sister's name is Johnni Hankins."

Michael removed a small notepad and pen from his coat pocket. As he wrote down the name, he glanced back at Julie. "Is that her married name or her maiden name?"

"Maiden name. Johnni never grew up, really."

Michael made another note. "Do you happen to have a photograph of your sister?"

"A photograph?" she repeated, staring at Michael.

"I understand you've been separated since you were young. I just thought—"

"Wait a minute. I do have something. Follow me."

Keeping an eye out for Lucifer, Michael cautiously followed the tiny woman back through the door and across the hall to a large room with cream-colored walls and red accents in oriental rug, love seat, and chair. A coffee table held an assortment of pictures. At the far end of the room, an easel was placed beside a table holding small pots of paint and charcoal pencils in a ceramic jar. Beyond the easel, a glass wall overlooked a wide expanse of meadow that ended at the edge of the woods.

"Nice view," he said, admitting to himself for the first time how beautiful the land was in this area. He had closed his eyes to the beauty when he came to Oak Shadows with Elizabeth, but now, begrudgingly, he could see why she was pulled back to her roots.

"After we married, Malcomb converted this room into a studio for me," Julie said.

Michael walked over to look through the glass window. A doe had come out of the woods to feed on the edge of the meadow. It was nice to think about Katie seeing wildlife in her backyard, yet he worried about their safety in this remote area.

"Oh, you see the doe out there?" Julie asked softly, as though using a loud voice would scare the deer away. He glanced back at Julie, thinking how like the doe Julie was. Vulnerable. Cautious. Wary of people.

"Malcomb planted green fields for deer and hired a biologist to establish a quail habitat," she said, looking thoughtful as she watched the deer feeding.

Michael nodded, looking over the impressive landscape. "Good idea."

"You want to follow me into the kitchen? I have to check on the chicken."

It was late for lunch, Michael realized, but the smell of chicken brought a growl to his stomach that he hoped Julie Waterford hadn't heard.

He followed her into the kitchen, a large, country-style room with lots of copper and brass. White woven baskets decorated the wall. She had gone to the stove to lift the lid on a skillet.

"You do your own cooking?" he asked, glancing around the empty kitchen.

"I like to cook," she said, lifting a long-handled fork to turn the pieces of chicken. "I learned a lot from Bessie. She was our closest neighbor up at Woodfield. A wonderful black woman. Johnni and I used to love to hang out in her kitchen." She replaced the lid and lowered the heat.

Michael had discreetly made another note in his notebook.

"You asked about a picture," she reminded him, leading the way back to her studio. She leaned over the coffee table where several pictures were displayed. She selected one with an antique frame. "Here's Johnni. It's the only picture I have."

Two little girls dressed in playsuits stood in front of a gray shack. One girl had brown hair and dark eyes, the other girl

61

had striking red hair and green eyes.

"I can't tell much about her," Michael said, tilting the photograph toward the light for a better look.

"I wish I could do a sketch for you, but I'm only good at abstracts," Julie said with a sigh.

Looking from the picture back to Julie, he could see a resemblance in facial features. "I think you two favor each other a bit."

Julie bit her lip, staring at the picture. "Our features are similar, but our coloring is different, as you can see. And our personalities. I tend to be as shy as a mouse. Johnni has never been afraid of anything except..." Her voice trailed off as she took the photo from Michael, then walked over to the coffee table, replacing the picture.

"Except what?" Michael prompted.

"I'd rather not talk about the man who fathered us," she said in a barely audible voice.

"Okay." Michael nodded, pursing his lips. *That's what you pay my wife to listen to,* he thought, wishing he didn't feel so bitter about Elizabeth's work. He tried not to think about what Anita had said, but he knew it was true. They were both devoted to their jobs, and those jobs had eventually wedged their way into the heart of their marriage, absorbing all of their spare time—time they should have spent together.

"Any other sisters or brothers?" he asked, pushing his mind back to Julie's family.

"No. The seventeen-year-old girl who gave birth to us died when we were two years old. I doubt that she ever had proper medical care. We were very poor. We were raised in a shack on the Coosa River, in a little community known as Woodfield. It's not far from Rome, Georgia."

Michael looked at her. "That's northwest Georgia; I was born and raised in northeast Georgia. Moonglow."

"Moonglow." She spoke the name softly. "That sounds pretty. There's nothing pretty about Woodfield. It's just as the name implies—woods and fields. It's a very small town."

Michael looked back at the name on his notepad. "I understand you and your sister were separated when you were eight years old."

Julie took a deep, long breath and turned to face the glass window. The doe was gone now, but she continued to stare at the meadow. "I was fortunate enough to be adopted by wonderful people. Johnni had a terrible life." She fell silent, as though lost in thought. "I had not heard from her in years," she said, her voice a monotone. "Then, shortly after Malcomb died, the phone rang one day, and it was Johnni. 'I've found you,' she said."

Julie's brown eyes lit up for a moment as she spoke of finding her sister again. Michael could see that she would be an attractive woman if only there were any light in her face.

"I was so lonely. Naturally, when I heard Johnni's voice, I was thrilled. But as we talked, I began to see what the years had done to her. She had grown very cynical." She ran a hand through her short hair and began to pace the floor. "She refused to talk about her personal life, so I didn't press her. But she became angry, quarrelsome. She said some terrible things to me." She closed her eyes for a moment, swaying slightly.

Michael reached out to steady her. "Hey, are you okay?"

She nodded. "I'm okay. I have to be okay."

"Do you think your sister is in Atlanta?" he asked, glancing again at the photograph.

"I don't know. I think so, although she wouldn't leave an address or phone number." She turned her eyes back to him as a curious look slipped over her features. "You actually think you could find her?"

"I specialize in finding missing people," he said, trying

to sound reassuring, although she was giving him very little to go on.

"You might start your search at the Peachtree Hotel," Julie said, chewing her lip and staring at something on the table. "She called from a bar there when she—" Her voice broke as some dark memory appeared to seize her.

"Go on," he prompted, jotting down the hotel in his notebook.

"That was the last time she called. She said, 'I just wanted you to know there's going to be an accident before our next birthday. You'd better be very careful.'"

"What do you think she meant?" Michael asked.

Julie shook her head, closing her eyes.

Michael could see the subject of her twin was painful to Julie. Elizabeth had her work cut out for her, that was for sure.

"Could you tell me more about your sister?"

"We both turn twenty-nine on October 11," she finally replied. "I believe she would be a beautiful woman. Her hair was a striking shade of red, like maples in the fall. It was her most distinguishing feature. And her eyes are a vivid green. She has an oval face like mine, and she was fortunate enough not to have freckles, despite the red hair."

A thought occurred to Michael. "Do you have a recent photograph of yourself? Just in case she still bears a resemblance to you?"

Again, Julie looked startled. "Why, yes. But how would that help you?" she asked, obviously puzzled.

He shrugged, recalling other cases where he had used a police artist's sketch to track someone down. "I'll make a copy of your picture and return it to you. I'll use the copy and get a sketch artist to change the color of the hair and eyes. Who knows? It might not work, but for now it's all we have. Does she have any scars or distinguishing features?"

Julie shrugged. "She had none the last time I saw her. But she may have changed a lot now. She may not look like me at all."

"Maybe I'll get lucky," he said, to encourage her. "Maybe there's still enough resemblance that someone at the Peachtree Hotel will remember her. Maybe she still goes there. I follow all leads."

She still looked puzzled as they walked back to the den and she picked up a five-by-seven color photograph. She handed it to Michael.

Michael studied the picture. The photograph featured a woman who looked quite different from the one he had met today. Her short brown hair was neatly waved, her face held a light covering of makeup, and an expression of happiness lit her brown eyes. Losing her husband had almost destroyed Julie Waterford, Michael decided—that and her sister taunting her so cruelly. His eyes scanned the white Georgian blouse she wore in the photograph, then returned to the small woman standing at a distance from him.

"That picture was made a year ago," she said, nodding toward the photograph he held.

"That's fine. I think it will be helpful, and I'll return it to you as soon as possible."

"It doesn't matter," she said, her voice toneless.

"Well, it was nice meeting you." Michael smiled at her and started toward the door.

"Wait!"

He turned back, startled by the urgency in her voice. "I don't know what kind of people she hangs out with...." Her features had that pinched expression once again. The woman in the picture and the one hugging the white Persian tightly against her were quite different. Michael now understood why Elizabeth had said Julie Waterford was a woman on the brink of a breakdown. "Be careful," she said, looking worried.

"Don't worry about me," he said reassuringly. "I'll be okay. And I'll call you in a couple of days."

She appeared to be forcing a smile, but her lips looked stiff, tense. "You have a lovely wife," she said, opening the door for him. Her eyes drifted to the driveway, then swung to the left, toward the woods. Beyond the narrow line of woods, Elizabeth's land began.

He took a deep breath, feeling a sudden rush of pain well up in his heart. "Thank you," he said, unsure of any other way to respond. "Well, again, it was nice meeting you. Try not to worry," he added, then felt silly for the remark.

He hurried back to his car and got in, starting the engine. He thought of Katie and wondered if he should drive on over and see her. Glancing at his watch, he realized it was not yet time for her to get out of school. But Elizabeth was probably home. As he reached the end of the driveway, he braked and stared bewildered at the road before him. Should he turn right and drive back into Atlanta? Or should he turn left, drive up to Oak Shadows, and have a talk with Elizabeth?

He sat staring blankly at the road, torn with conflict. He still loved Elizabeth. He always would. But there was so much to settle between them....

Seven

Michael sat in his car for a long time, lost in thought, unable to make a decision. Then he remembered something Katie had mentioned to him over the weekend: Something was wrong with the chain on her bicycle. He had tossed some new chains in the backseat yesterday.

Glancing again at his watch, he realized it was about time for Katie to get out of school. Since he had the chains anyway, he really should venture over and repair the broken chain for her. Or, at least he could check it out. There might be more wrong with her bike than a messed-up chain, knowing Katie.

He turned and drove toward the house, trying to blind himself to the beauty of the oaks and maples, which were starting to turn. In a few weeks, the trees would evolve into a brilliant array of color. It would be quite spectacular. And yes—Oak Shadows would be a nice place to grow up, provided you had lots of money for upkeep, which Elizabeth had acquired through a trust fund. Strange, he thought, steering the car up the driveway, that this factor had to evolve into such a problem between them, when once they had been so crazy in love.

He saw as he reached the house that Elizabeth's car was gone. *Good,* he told himself, trying to focus on the relief he felt and not on the disappointment that also nagged him. He could check out the bike and be gone before they got home, thus avoiding another confrontation with Elizabeth. He reached for the package that contained new chains and got out of the car.

He found the bike out back of the house, propped against the porch, where Katie said she usually parked it. Elizabeth, in her usual neatness, had left an old towel there, and apparently Katie had made the most of it. There was grease all over the towel.

He examined the bike and saw that the problem was, indeed, a worn-out chain. He could have the old chain off and a new one replaced in no time.

Soon he was gripping the handlebars, pushing the bike back and forth, testing the chain. No problem now. He reached for the towel and was wiping his hands when he heard the sound of a car in the front driveway.

He walked around the side of the house in time to see Elizabeth and Katie getting out of the white Honda.

"Dad!" Katie bounded toward him.

"You were right," he said, still wiping his hands. "It was the chain. Want to see if the chain holds now?"

"Oh, Dad. Thanks a bunch." She raced around the side of the house for a ride on her bike.

"Wait, Katie," her mother called. "Your old jeans, please."

With a resentful groan, Katie flounced up the front porch steps. Michael noted the nice-looking slacks set Katie was wearing. It was good that Elizabeth paid attention to detail. He wouldn't have stopped her, and she could have ended up with grease smears on her new clothes.

He stood facing Elizabeth. She was wearing a white linen jacket over a loose floral skirt. Her golden hair was styled in a straight loose wave that brushed her shoulders. The simple small gold hoop earrings he had given her two years ago glinted in the afternoon sunshine that slanted over her face. He was struck, all over again, at how her simple, natural beauty appealed to him.

He forced his eyes back to the towel, wiping the last traces of bicycle grease away.

"Want to come inside and wash up?" she asked.

"No, this got it." He finished wiping his hands on the towel, then laid it on the front porch. "I just left Julie Waterford's place," he said, glancing back at Elizabeth.

Elizabeth looked pleased, her bracelet of car keys dangling from her wrist. He noticed this, as he noticed everything else, and recalled how he had gone to a hardware store near their town house in Atlanta to look for a key chain she couldn't lose.

She dropped down in a rocking chair on the porch and gestured to one for him. "Thanks for going. Tell me about it."

He shrugged. "She's nice but quite shy."

Elizabeth nodded. "Yeah. One reason is, she developed agoraphobia after the doctor died. Agoraphobia usually follows trauma. She misses Dr. Waterford terribly." She took a deep breath, gazing out across the front lawn. "Dr. Waterford was a genius. I've read some of his papers."

"Apparently, her sister would have been a hot topic for one of those papers."

Elizabeth's mouth tilted in a half-smile. "It seems that way, doesn't it? Welfare took them when they were young. They were adopted separately. Julie hasn't seen her twin in years. Now Johnni has looked her up and is doing some weird stuff."

"What's really weird," Michael commented, "is that Johnni knows how to find Julie, but Julie can't find Johnni."

"Dad, are you trying to make a riddle?" Katie asked, bursting onto the front porch.

Michael laughed. "Not really."

Just then his beeper sounded, and he checked the call. It was the number of an important client.

"I have to make a call, but I can do it from my car phone on the way back."

"Do you have to leave?" Katie asked, clearly disappointed.

Michael sighed. "I'm afraid so. I'm searching for a missing child, and I may have a lead. Which is one reason I need to stay in Atlanta," he said casually, hoping to reinforce his position with both of them.

Elizabeth's brown eyes flashed with anger at that reminder, but he ignored her expression as he gave Katie a quick kiss and hurried toward his car. "Talk to you later."

Once inside, he dialed the number on his phone and learned from Tom Murphy that a call had come in from his daughter. He now suspected that her mother had taken her to another state.

He accelerated the car, taking the curves at full speed. In the meantime, he called his office and alerted Anita.

"Anita, I'm up in the country. Please locate Lee and tell him to get to the Murphy house right away," he informed her.

Lee was a top-notch investigator who worked for Michael.

As he sped back to the city, he tried to concentrate on the Murphy case, but Elizabeth kept cropping up in his mind. Today he had realized the extent of her knowledge of mental disorders when she spoke of Julie. Why couldn't he bring himself to voice his appreciation to Elizabeth? Somewhere in the depths of his heart it occurred to him that he was still trying to punish her. And he suddenly felt as small and hardheaded as a kid being told he couldn't have his way.

Eight

Tuesday, October 1

Elizabeth was seated at her desk, her hands folded over the blotter, her attention focused on the tall, stout woman in her sixties who sat wiping her eyes with a lace handkerchief.

"Grief is such a hard thing to handle, but you've helped me a lot, Elizabeth."

Elizabeth shook her head slowly. "All I've done is suggest that you begin every day with a devotion, center your thoughts on God's care, and then pray for the strength to face that day." She smiled. "After all, we can only live one day at a time."

The woman replaced her glasses and folded her handkerchief, staring at it for a moment before returning it to the leather handbag in her lap. "You're right. And before I began those early morning devotions, each day was—" she shook her head slowly, fighting tears again—"Almost unbearable. Howard and I had been together for thirty-nine years. And there are no children to ease the loss."

Elizabeth bit her lip, fighting tears of her own. As the woman spoke, she found herself thinking of Katie, of course, and ultimately of Michael. Were they wasting precious time together by being willful and stubborn? After all, no one had an assurance of how long his or her time on earth would be. Life was a suspension bridge from birth to death—and one had limited control of the bridge. Any day it could snap.

"Well, my hour is up." Lucille Tyler came to her feet, forcing Elizabeth back to the reality of the moment. She stood, too. Her eyes swept down the woman, and she couldn't help noting how capable and in control she appeared once she squared her shoulders and looked you straight in the eye. *The heart is so fragile*, Elizabeth thought, trying to force a smile. She felt shaky herself.

"Do you want to come again next week at this same time?" she asked, belatedly remembering her ledger of appointments.

"I would prefer to change the time to Wednesday at four, if that suits you. That way I can leave from here and go on to the church and help out with covered-dish suppers before prayer meeting."

Elizabeth nodded. "Katie and I hope to get started on Wednesday evenings soon. She's still getting adjusted to the change in schools, and we've been getting bogged down with homework. She's doing pretty well in most things, but math is not her strong point," she said, shaking her head.

"Well, it's been wonderful having the two of you on Sundays," Lucille said, looking relaxed once again.

The two of you. It seemed so odd to be attending church without Michael. Thank God, most people were tactful in not asking about the missing husband and father, although she knew Michael kept up his attendance at their church in Atlanta.

She followed Lucille to the door, trying to force her thoughts toward picking up Katie. "Have a good week," she said, touching her lightly on the shoulder.

"Thanks. You too," the woman called as she hurried out the

door and down the steps to her blue Buick.

Elizabeth closed the door and leaned against it, allowing herself the luxury of just a few more minutes of reflection. Lucille's words had struck a raw nerve, and now Elizabeth debated again the wisdom of moving here to Oak Shadows and leaving Michael behind in Atlanta. But then, she reminded herself, they had spent little time together toward the end. Both were obsessed with their work, blocking their communication to the point that they had finally stopped talking completely. And one day they awoke to find themselves feeling like strangers living together, functioning as a family, yet separated by a deep chasm.

God, help us to work this out, Elizabeth prayed silently as she stared into space. Michael's mother had been so kind, so tactful when she brought Katie back on Sunday afternoon. Elizabeth had always loved her mother-in-law, who managed to always be there for her daughter-in-law and granddaughter without giving advice or asking questions, although Elizabeth knew the temptation must be great.

She sighed. No more time for reflection. School would be out in ten minutes. She grabbed her shoulder bag, which was looped around a hook on the hall tree, then turned to the marble-topped table and reached into the dish for her car keys.

Michael hurried down the busy corridor of the office complex, seeking the right door. He found it quickly, for he came here often. Turning inside, he stepped up to the long counter, looking across at the beehive of desks and secretaries. Tina, an attractive woman with coffee brown skin and deep brown eyes, stood at the end of the counter, filling out a form for an elderly man. Michael worked his way down the counter, waiting patiently until the man thanked her and left.

"Hi, Tina," he greeted her.

"Michael, where have you been?"

"Running in circles. How's it going?"

"Great," she said with a brilliant smile. "Tommy and I are expecting a baby next March." Absently, she rubbed the simple gold band on her left hand. "We can't wait for our baby."

"Hey, that's wonderful, Tina," he said, glad to see the happiness shining from her dark eyes. "I've never met your husband. Maybe sometime the three of us could have lunch."

She sighed. "I never see him for lunch anymore. He works as a repairman at a computer shop, then goes to school at night. Now he may have to pick up extra weekend work to help out with expenses, since there's a baby on the way. How can I help you?"

Michael took a step closer, lowering his voice. "I need a favor, Tina."

Tina cocked a dark eyebrow and shook her curly hair. "You're overdrawn on favors, Michael."

"Then how about dinner for you and Tommy?"

Tina grinned. "That would be nice. Or how about a weekend job for Tommy? Isn't there something he could do to help you find missing people?"

Michael thought it over. "As a matter of fact, I could use a stakeout guy. Would he go for that?"

"Probably. He loves intrigue," she said with a laugh.

Michael nodded, the matter settled for now. "Then I'd like to talk with him. Why don't you and Tommy meet me after work when it's convenient? I'm serious about dinner."

"Sounds great." An amused twinkle filled her dark eyes. "Now what was it you needed?"

"Tina, could you run the name Johnni Hankins through your files?"

Tina shook her head and clucked her tongue, but she continued to smile at him. "Poor Michael, always on the search. Which files am I perusing this time?"

"Driver's license, motor-vehicle registration, anything to help me turn up a missing person. Come on, Tina. You're so good at your work; I shouldn't have to detail it."

"You promise to hire Tommy?"

Michael sensed she was still teasing him, but he was serious. "I really do need a stakeout guy. When can you two meet me?"

"As a matter of fact, he's out of school tomorrow evening, so we had planned to do some shopping after work. Wanna join us for a hamburger?"

Michael mentally ran through the next day's schedule and nodded. "That'll work out. Want to meet me in the lobby of the Peachtree Hotel?"

She cocked an eyebrow. "I said a hamburger. You're talking a real dinner if it's the Peachtree."

"It'll be my pleasure. Six o'clock okay?"

"Fine with me. Maybe I'll have your information by then."

He winked. "Thanks, Tina."

Michael hurried out. Tina and her husband lived on a shoe-string, yet she looked deliriously happy. Just as he and Elizabeth had been in the beginning. He recalled Tina's simple gold band, symbolizing an unbroken circle. How many weeks had he spent shopping for Elizabeth's ring? He had wanted her to have the best, but on his salary the best was impossible. Finally, he had located a quality stone at a jeweler who was generous with credit. It took him a year to pay off the debt, but Elizabeth loved the ring. And even her mother, an expert on fine jewelry, approved of his choice.

He grinned bitterly as he pushed through the revolving door, moved quickly down the steps, and headed for the parking lot. If only her mother had approved of him the way she did his ring! But she had set her sights on someone of equal

75

status for Elizabeth. A physician, an attorney.

He shook his head. He was being childish and trite to entertain such thoughts. But Elizabeth seemed to be picking up where her mother had left off, silently watching him with critical eyes, wanting more than he could give her. And of course his pride kept getting in the way. His mother had reminded him yesterday that he was a wonderful guy—he just needed to pray about the two qualities that were affecting his marriage: pride and stubbornness.

And Mom is usually right, he admitted to himself as his footsteps quickened across the concrete of the parking lot. Looking around, he tried to change the direction of his thoughts, yet he seemed to be stuck in the same old groove of resentment. Obviously, he just wasn't prosperous enough for Elizabeth. She had to keep going to school, insuring herself of a job that would make her financially secure. He bumped into a small elderly man shuffling toward the parking lot.

"Oops, sorry, sir," Michael said, bracing the tottering man.

"You'd better slow down, young man," the man said, but with a laugh.

Michael forced a polite laugh in return, trying to regain his sense of humor. Glancing at his watch, he noted that it was almost five. Offices would soon be closing. He'd get a fresh start tomorrow with the sketch artist. Maybe Johnni Hankins still resembled her twin sister. Though there were exceptions, generally facial features didn't change that much. He had decided his best chance at finding Johnni was to have the artist copy Julie's picture and change the hair and eyes, maybe giving a more sensual look to the face. And a different blouse. From what he had heard of Johnni, she wouldn't be dressed in a proper white blouse like the one Julie wore in the picture.

Unlocking the door to his Jeep, he shook his head. It was very likely that he was on a wild-goose chase. But something

Johnni Hankins had told her sister kept haunting him....

I just wanted you to know there's going to be an accident before our next birthday. You'd better be very careful.

What strange, taunting words. The fact that Malcomb Waterford had died in a car accident didn't calm his nerves in the least. He had a feeling he was dealing with a very dangerous woman.

Nine

A sheet of gray rain drifted down over Atlanta, clogging the late-evening traffic along Peachtree, as a taxi pulled to the curb before Dailey's and a slim redhead emerged.

Johnni Hankins opened her white umbrella, a perfect match for the white satin raincoat, and walked briskly up the steps. A man at the door rushed to assist her, opening the door wide and greeting her with a friendly smile.

"Thanks." She gave him a provocative grin and hurried inside.

The man stared after her, wishing he were not late for an appointment. After all, she was a beautiful woman with an interesting shade of red hair and lovely green eyes that flashed her appreciation. Sighing with regret over the appointment he couldn't break, he closed the door behind her and descended the steps.

Inside Dailey's, a popular restaurant and lounge, the evening crowd had gathered as Johnni placed her umbrella in a rack and headed toward the lounge.

As she slipped to a secluded table in the corner, her eyes

flew over the crowd as if seeking just the right person. Couples sat at tables, talking in low voices. The mirrored bar nearby reflected an array of bottles and glasses, and several businessmen perched on barstools.

"What'll you have, miss?" A cocktail waitress stood at the table, distracting Johnni momentarily.

She looked at the waitress and shrugged. "Just a glass of white wine," she answered.

Her eyes returned to the businessmen at the bar.

Ten

Wednesday, October 2

Katie was happy today. She loved being out-of-doors, and the teacher had promised a leaf hunt this afternoon. Yanking her overalls on over her T-shirt, she grabbed her book bag. She hesitated before her dresser mirror, checking her appearance to save time. If something was wrong, her mother would send her back upstairs. She had carefully brushed her blonde hair, scrubbed her face, and brushed her teeth hard after the cereal and juice. Now Mom would approve and drive her to school. Brooke would be waiting for her.

Hooking her book bag over her shoulder, she ran out the door and down the stairs.

"Mom," she called out. She saw her mother on the front porch deep in conversation with a man dressed in white pants and shirt, wearing a baseball cap. He was saying something about paint.

"I don't know where to start." Her mother shook her head, looking from the front of the house back to the man. All the while, she picked at her nails the way she did when she got nervous. Then her eyes met Katie's, and she glanced at her watch. "Oh, my goodness. I have to get my daughter to school. You're welcome to stay and poke around the outside of the house and see what you think needs to be done."

The man removed his baseball cap and scratched his head. "Quite a lot, I'm afraid."

"I'll be back in about fifteen minutes," she said, her hand on Katie's shoulder as they hurried to the car.

"Are we really gonna live out here for good, Mom?" Katie asked, once they were settled into their white Honda.

"Buckle your seat belt," Elizabeth reminded her as she turned the key in the ignition. "The house has to be redone anyway, Katie, so why not live here for a while and see how it goes? You like school, don't you?"

Katie nodded. Now that she had adjusted to the small public school, she had to admit that she preferred it over the private school she had attended in Atlanta. "It's just that…" She hesitated, glancing at her mother.

"What?" Elizabeth asked absently, peering down the driveway canopied with century-old oaks.

"I miss Dad," Katie said in a small voice. It was useless to say it again, but she couldn't make the ache go away. She did miss her dad, and when she was with him, she missed her mom. Why couldn't grownups work out their silly old problems?

"Well, maybe in time…" Elizabeth's voice trailed off as she steered the car onto the two-lane country road that ran past oak woods, meadows, sleepy cottages, and sprawling farms.

"Maybe in time *what*?" Katie pressed. Hope was springing back into her heart as she turned toward her mother.

"Maybe in time, God will work things out," Elizabeth finally replied.

They sped past the turnoff to Waterford Farm and Katie noticed that her mother had gotten real quiet, like she was deep in thought. Katie leaned back against the seat, staring at the blue sky overhead. Her thoughts turned to her school day. She liked her new teacher, Mrs. Abrams, who always gave them an opportunity to be out-of-doors when the weather was pretty. Katie was glad it was a pretty day.

Elizabeth was thinking of Julie's phone call Monday evening. She had phoned just after dinner to inform Elizabeth of Michael's visit. She took a deep breath, recalling the rest of Julie's conversation.

"I was impressed by his kindness and sincerity," Julie had commented, "but I honestly don't think he can find Johnni." Her voice sounded weary, hopeless.

"Give him a chance," Elizabeth told her. "And anytime you'd like to come over for a cup of tea or coffee, it doesn't have to be an official visit. I get lonely too."

Julie made some reply that indicated she appreciated the offer, but underneath the words, Elizabeth sensed a wariness. As though she preferred being alone.

Could Michael find Johnni before the twins' next birthday, October 11, which was a week from Friday? If he didn't find her, would this crazy Johnni carry out her threat? Perhaps it was no more than a threat; still, the word *accident* had been a dangerous one to use, considering Dr. Malcomb Waterford's car wreck. *And how thoroughly was that car wreck investigated?* she wondered suddenly, chewing on her lip as she turned into the driveway to Katie's school.

Michael stood beside the sketch artist, who was shaking his head. "It's hard to picture this lady as a flaming redhead, but I'll give it my best shot."

"I know you will," Michael said. He had always respected Chuck's work. He was very good, and his sketches usually paid off.

Chuck's hand moved swiftly over the paper, outlining an oval face, adding small features. Michael watched, amazed at his talent.

"Green eyes, you said?" Chuck asked.

"Emerald green."

"The hair is light red? Dark red?"

"I'm not sure. Let's try a medium red."

"Long or short?"

Michael shook his head uncertainly, feeling his frustration mount. He realized what a wild-goose chase he was on, but it was too late to back out now.

"I don't know, Chuck. Can you just put a modern hairstyle on her?"

Chuck pursed his lip, thinking. "How old did you say she is?"

Michael sighed. "She's almost twenty-nine."

Chuck stared at the sketch. "My sister is thirty. She has one of those short hairstyles. Want me to make this hairstyle short?"

"Whatever you think." His mind had darted back to Elizabeth's long blonde hair, worn in a straight casual style. But this woman was nothing like Elizabeth. He thought of Julie. Twins were supposed to be somewhat similar, but these two appeared to be as far apart as daylight and dark. "The other sister wears her hair short. Yeah, make it short," he decided.

"That feels right," the artist answered vaguely, as though he were only half listening.

Michael watched Chuck's artistry in motion as a beautiful version of Julie emerged on canvas. He caught his breath, all of his instincts telling him Johnni looked very similar to this sketch.

84

"I don't see how you do it, Chuck." Michael tapped his shoulder. "I'm always amazed by your talent."

"Thanks. Who is this woman, by the way?"

"Her name is Johnni Hankins. If you see her, there'll be a reward."

"No reward necessary, other than the usual fee." He grinned at Michael.

"You may even get a bonus this time. Thanks, pal."

Michael entered the atrium lobby of the Peachtree Hotel and looked around. Across the crowded lobby, he spotted Tina and headed in her direction.

Tina and her husband were walking around, hand in hand, looking over the plush interior of the hotel. She glanced back over her shoulder, spotted Michael, and began to wave. He quickened his steps to catch up with them.

"Hi. You must be Tommy?" Michael extended his hand to the tall, thirty-something guy. He wore khakis and a white sweater, contrasting nicely with his dark skin.

"Tommy Kline. And you're Michael Calloway."

"Now that you two have met—" Tina looked from one man to the other—"I'll deliver the bad news, Michael." She shook her head, looking regretful. "There's nothing on your missing lady. She doesn't drive a car, vote, or own property. She only exists in your dreams."

Michael gave a sardonic laugh. "She exists. She must be using a married name."

He withdrew a sketch from his pocket. He had stopped at an office-supply shop to duplicate the original, and now he was armed with copies of Chuck's sketch. "Here she is."

Both Tommy and Tina studied the picture.

"Yep, Tina, this is the perfect job for me."

Tina landed a playful punch on Tommy's shoulder. He merely laughed at her response to his joke.

"She's a pretty lady," Tina said, more seriously. "But maybe she's not in Atlanta."

"If she is, I bet she's hanging out in Buckhead," Tommy said, looking back at Michael.

Michael nodded. "That's possible." His eyes scanned the lobby of the hotel. "Her sister said she called from a bar here."

"*Here?*" Tina asked, turning to scan the distinguished-looking people walking purposefully across the lobby to check into the hotel.

"She probably called from the Sun Dial lounge on top." Tommy gestured to an upper floor.

"Well, let's have dinner," Michael said. "I'll wait until after we eat to check that place out. You two hungry?"

"Tina's always hungry." Tommy laughed.

"Got to keep the little one fed," she said, patting her stomach.

Michael smiled down at her. "You don't look like there's a little one on the way."

"Trust me, there is."

Tommy nudged Michael. "We heard the heartbeat today."

Tenderness filled Michael as he recalled how special that moment had been for Elizabeth and himself. "Congratulations, again." He looked from one to the other. "There's no feeling in the world like being a parent."

"How's your little daughter?" Tina asked brightly.

"Fine," he answered, without missing a beat. Not everyone knew that he and Elizabeth were separated, and he tried to avoid the subject whenever possible.

"Would you be interested in a part-time job, Tommy?" Michael asked. In the few minutes of their conversation, he had decided Tommy was a sharp guy, and quite perceptive. The kind of employee he liked having around.

"Sure would."

Michael nodded, leading the way. "We'll talk about it over dinner."

Eleven

A fter dinner and good-byes to Tina and Tommy, Michael stepped off the elevator into the Sun Dial lounge, a revolving bar on the seventy-second floor, overlooking Atlanta. Michael walked over to a window, staring out at the spectacular view of the city's night lights. Looking down, the neon setting against the darkness reminded him of a black velvet canvas dotted with twinkling diamonds, rubies, and emeralds. It was a beautiful picture of the city he loved.

A hostess approached him. She was an attractive brunette in her early thirties. "May I help you, sir?"

"I won't be staying," he answered politely. "But I *am* looking for someone."

A smile tilted the corners of her mouth. "Oh, you are?"

"My name is Michael Calloway, and I have a detective agency, Searchers." He removed a business card from his wallet and handed it to the hostess. Then he showed her a copy of Johnni's sketch. "Her family is worried about her. Her name is Johnni Hankins. Or rather, that was her maiden name. I'm not sure about the last name now."

The hostess studied the sketch for a moment; then she began to nod. "There has been a lady in here a couple of times who resembles this one. The hairstyle was different."

"How so?" Michael asked, feeling a glimmer of hope.

"A more modern look to her. Her hair was a short shag." She pursed her lips. "But the facial features were very similar. Yes, I think it might be the same woman."

"Could you tell me more about her, please? Her sister needs to get in touch with her. It's very important," he added, hoping to convey the urgency of finding her.

"Let's see." The hostess hesitated, studying the picture again. "I remember she was dressed well and wore expensive jewelry."

Michael nodded. "Was she alone or with someone?"

She studied the picture again. "I'm almost certain she came alone," she replied, slowly, "but I believe she left with a man. That was the last time she was in."

"Do you know the man?" Michael asked hopefully.

She shook her head. "Never saw him before or since. The other time she came in, I was just leaving. In fact, I nearly bumped into her at the elevator. But she didn't seem to notice me. It was obvious—" She bit off the comment she was about to make.

"What was obvious?" Michael prompted.

"Well, you know how it goes. A single woman looking for a man," she answered with a little smile.

"You think she came here to meet men?"

She shrugged. "Mr. Calloway, she wouldn't be the first one. I hope you find her if her family is worried, but she seemed fine to me."

"Could I persuade you to call me if she returns?"

She hesitated. "Maybe. But I have to warn you, our management frowns upon violating the privacy of our customers."

Michael looked into her eyes and said, quite seriously, "We

have a problem with this woman. We don't want this problem to escalate to a police matter."

"No, we don't," she said, understanding the implications. "Okay, I'll call you if she comes back." She tapped the business card against the back of her hand, then glanced down at it again. "Your home phone is here too. Good. I don't know when I might see her. What if it's quite late?"

"Call anytime. Please."

"Okay. By the way, my name is Marty."

"Thanks, Marty."

He smiled and walked away, feeling as though he had finally accomplished something. As he pressed the elevator button, he tried to imagine Johnni stepping off the elevator, bumping into the hostess, yet strangely preoccupied. A single woman looking for a man, Marty had said. *Did she find one?* he wondered as he stepped on the elevator.

By the time he reached his apartment and unlocked the door, the weariness of another long day began to settle into his neck and shoulders. He was never sure if the tired feeling came from a long day or the knowledge that no one was waiting for him. He let himself in and turned on the light in the foyer. Through habit, he went straight for the phone, checking his messages. As usual, the little red light was blinking. He pressed the button.

"Hi, Michael, it's Jay. I wanted to invite you to come with me to a small-group meeting of Promise Keepers tomorrow evening. Unless you're knee-deep in a case, I won't take no for an answer. Meet me at that restaurant near your office at five o'clock. We'll grab a bite and go from there."

Jay's message was the only one on the machine. Michael turned and headed for the kitchen. Promise Keepers. He had been hearing good things about this men's organization, but being separated from his wife and child made him feel out of place in a gathering like that. Just staying in church was a chore, to sit alone week after week in that special place at the end of a pew he had shared with Elizabeth and Katie.

He turned on the kitchen light, opened the door to an empty refrigerator, and reached for a small carton of milk. If Katie were here, he would make hot chocolate for the two of them. Tonight, he'd settle for a cold glass of milk. As he opened the cabinet for a glass, he began to think of Jay and Tracy and how happy they were since they married.

Tracy had moved back to Atlanta before the wedding, got a job with CNN, and she and Jay now shared a cute little place in Buckhead. They went to the lake or to Moonglow lots of weekends. Even though they both enjoyed their work, their marriage came first. *Jay is so in love*, Michael thought, pouring the milk, smiling at the thought of his younger brother, happy at last.

The problem was, Jay and Tracy were inseparable when not at work, and he rarely saw Jay anymore.

Michael finished the milk and set the glass down. If nothing big came up tomorrow, maybe he'd tag along to the meeting of Promise Keepers. At least it would give him a chance to spend some time with Jay. He hadn't seen him in weeks.

Jay had said that he wouldn't take no for an answer, that he'd meet him after work. Michael had to be in court all day, but he could leave the courthouse and go directly to the restaurant near his office. For once, he wouldn't make a dash back to the office after court. That would be a relief.

CHAPTER

Twelve

Thursday, October 3

"C oming!" Elizabeth yelled at the phone in her office as it continued to ring. She had dropped Katie off at school, suffered through another session with the frustrated painter, then thrown up her hands and called an interior decorator to come on Saturday. It was going to take more than money to redo Oak Shadows the way she wanted. It would take someone with professional know-how. Redecorating an antebellum home was definitely not her specialty.

"Hello," she answered, trying not to sound irritated by the persistent ringing of the phone.

"Elizabeth," a female voice whispered into the phone.

Elizabeth frowned, gripping the phone tighter. "Yes, who's speaking, please?" For a moment, her mind flashed back to a woman she had worked with in Atlanta who called at all hours.

"Eliza-beth…" The caller repeated her name, a sob breaking the word in half.

Elizabeth concentrated on the voice. It was someone she had met recently. "Julie?" she asked tentatively.

"I can't come tomorrow.… I'm sick.…" The sobs were more

controlled now, but she was still crying.

"Julie, what's happened?"

There was a momentary pause. "It's terrible."

"Tell me!" Elizabeth gripped the phone tighter.

There was another pause.

"Are you at home?" Elizabeth asked, then recalled that Julie never left home, never went anywhere.

"Yes...." Her voice sounded weak and frightened.

"I'll be right over," Elizabeth said, hanging up the phone and racing for her car keys.

While the adjoining farm was in walking distance, Elizabeth knew the sound of desperation when she heard it. Julie Waterford was desperate. Within minutes, Elizabeth had driven from her farm to Julie's and lurched her car to a halt in front of the house.

Julie stood in the yard, holding the black cat. Her face was deathly pale. She seemed to be in a daze.

Elizabeth jumped out of the car and rushed to her side.

"What is it, Julie?" she asked gently.

Julie was not wearing her glasses, and her eyes were red and swollen.

"It all started last night," Julie said as the black cat meowed and started to lick her hand. "Johnni called from a bar. She sounded drunk. Her tone was angry, belligerent. She started in about our childhood." She hugged the cat tighter as she spoke.

"She said I was always the pet, that she took the beatings for both of us...."

"Don't let her words upset you," Elizabeth said soothingly. "She was probably inebriated."

The black cat had narrowed its yellow eyes toward Elizabeth and now leaped from Julie's arms to scamper around the side of the house.

"This morning I awoke with a terrible headache," Julie con-

94

tinued, her voice a monotone. "I took a long walk to the back of the property, hoping the fresh air would help. I was gone about an hour. I lay down under a tree and fell asleep." She looked up at Elizabeth, her brown eyes huge as fresh tears filled her eyes and spilled onto her cheeks.

"Come on inside. I'll show you why I'm upset."

Elizabeth followed Julie up the porch steps and entered the house. In the foyer, Elizabeth came up short, staring at the wall. Julie's abstract painting had been slashed. The canvas had been slashed to confetti.

"And look in here." Julie walked unsteadily toward the den.

Books had been raked from the bookshelves in wild abandon across the carpet. Sofa pillows were tossed about and, worst of all, the glass on Malcomb Waterford's portrait had been smashed.

Elizabeth sighed with relief that the portrait at least was still intact, unlike the abstract painting in the hall.

"What about the other rooms?" she asked, trying to sound calm.

"She didn't bother anything else downstairs. Not even the studio where I do my art. But upstairs…"

"Could you show me?"

Julie, nodded, leading the way up the winding stairs,

"Look, don't you think it's time to bring in the police?" Elizabeth asked, her worry showing despite herself.

"No!"

Elizabeth followed her up the stairs and down a carpeted corridor, scarcely noticing the lovely antiques. Why had Johnni done this? And why did Julie continue to defend her sister?

They entered a luxurious room with white French Provincial furnishings, crystal-beaded chandelier, white carpet, and white linen drapes.

Clothes were strewn from the mirrored doors of the closet

across the carpet and onto the bed. It was all a tumbled mess.

Elizabeth frowned, glancing at the variety of nice clothes.

"Is anything gone?" she asked, although she wondered how Julie could tell which clothes were missing when she had so many.

Julie picked up an empty, unzipped garment bag. "A couple of cocktail dresses that I bought for special functions I attended with Malcomb." Her eyes lifted past Elizabeth's head to some distant space. For a few moments, she seemed to be lost in memory.

"So she took two cocktail dresses," Elizabeth said, attempting to bring Julie back to the problem at hand.

Julie nodded, staring at the empty plastic bag. "When we were children, she did this. She'd paw through the few clothes I had. If she found something she wanted, she took it."

Elizabeth bit her lip, her thoughts muddled. "Julie, could this be a simple robbery? Are we jumping to the conclusion that the person who did this is your sister?"

Julie sighed. "She left her signature."

She walked to the doorway and stared into the adjoining room. Elizabeth followed, wondering what she'd see next.

The master bath was decorated in gold and white with a marble tub and a huge wall mirror over the vanity. In the center of the mirror, a large *J* was scrawled in vivid purple lipstick.

Elizabeth stared at the garish *J* in disbelief. What kind of sick woman were they dealing with?

Julie stood there, looking dazed as she spoke in a monotone. "Johnni used to take a bar of soap and write a *J* on our old cracked mirror back at the shack." She glanced at Elizabeth. "I thought it was some kind of home then, but the truth is, it was only a shack. Anyway, this is the kind of thing Johnni would do. She enjoyed being mischievous."

She turned away, as though sick at heart, and walked slowly

back into the bedroom. "When she was eight, she put a garden snake in bed with Bull and—"

"Bull?"

"That's the nickname she gave to the man who fathered us. It was appropriate; he was a bully. Anyway, she put a garden snake in bed with Bull. And one day the woman who was supposed to be baby-sitting us was having her usual long afternoon nap. She snored with her mouth open. Johnni went out to the yard, found a big worm, and dropped it in the woman's mouth."

Elizabeth stared in amazement. "You're telling me she was capable of these things when she was only eight?"

When Julie nodded in reply, Elizabeth's worries escalated. Michael had to find this woman. Not only was she sick, she was very dangerous. She had no doubt now that she would carry out her threats about an accident on the sisters' upcoming birthday.

"Yes, she was capable of those things at an early age," Julie answered the question, staring into space. "Johnni especially liked tormenting Bull. It was almost as if she wanted to be punished."

She removed a pill bottle from her pocket. "My migraine is starting up again. Excuse me." She returned to the bathroom, and the sound of water filled the silence as Elizabeth stood in the center of the bedroom, studying the tumbled mess.

"Julie, why does she want to torment you?" she called as her eyes roamed over the jumbled clothing.

"Like I told you before, she's jealous," Julie answered, returning to the bedroom. "She believes I've had all the things she's missed. And it's true. I have."

"But your life hasn't been easy. You've lost your husband. Surely—"

"You think Johnni feels compassion for me because of

Malcomb?" she asked, her brown eyes flashing bitterness. "She doesn't care about Malcomb. She only feels pain...and rage."

Elizabeth thought this over as they left the bedroom and descended the stairs to the first floor. Once they had reached the foyer, Elizabeth turned to Julie. "Are you sure you don't want to call the police?"

Julie hesitated for a few seconds, then began to shake her head. "I'm sure."

"Okay," Elizabeth sighed, "but from what I can see, we're dealing with a very sick woman. We have to find her, and soon. The police can put out an APB—"

"It will only make her worse. She's worse after she's punished."

This was one of the most bizarre cases Elizabeth had ever heard of. It reminded her of an abuse case in which the victim was unwilling to turn in the abuser. She had dealt with that in Atlanta.

Elizabeth shook her head, unable to follow Julie's logic.

"Then at least let me phone Michael."

Julie walked over to the desk and put on her glasses. "I guess that's okay."

"Good. I'll try to reach him now."

Elizabeth hurried to the desk phone, trying not to visibly wince at the awful mess. Reaching Michael was not as easy as she had hoped, however.

"Hi, Anita, this is Elizabeth. I need to speak with Michael."

"Sorry, Elizabeth." Anita's voice was warm and caring, as always. "He's in court today."

"What time do you expect him back?"

"Well, you know how trials can drag on, and he had to testify. When he left the office, he told me he probably wouldn't be back today."

Elizabeth sighed, wondering what to do. "Anita, this is very important. It has nothing to do with me or Katie—we're fine.

But I'm at the home of Julie Waterford, one of his clients. Her house has been broken into, and there is some serious vandalism here. Michael needs to come up as soon as possible."

"Oh, I see." Anita's tone changed, and Elizabeth could hear the sound of pages rustling. "I can try to beep him."

"I hate to interrupt him if he's testifying. Just leave word on his answering machine and a note on his desk. As soon as he's free, have him contact me. Thanks, Anita. Good talking with you."

"And it's always nice talking with you, Elizabeth."

As they said their good-byes and hung up, Elizabeth realized how much she had missed her daily chats with Anita. Elizabeth was always calling the office when she lived in town. Once a month, she tried to take Anita to lunch or have her come to the house. Anita lived alone and seemed to enjoy her conversations with Elizabeth and Michael, and she adored Katie.

She replaced the phone and felt her eyes drawn toward Malcomb Waterford's portrait. She had never met the man, but he was practically a legend in psychiatry, well respected for his work in many areas. Her eyes slipped back to Julie, who seemed more composed now. Elizabeth had a difficult time picturing Dr. Waterford and Julie together. *Opposites attract*, she reminded herself. And she imagined Julie was quite different before so much tragedy hit her.

"Is he driving up?" Julie asked, picking up her white cat, Angel, gently stroking her fur. She seemed more in control now as her eyes drifted over the room.

"Julie, Michael's in court today, but I've left a message. He'll call me tonight." Elizabeth ran her hand down the length of her blonde hair. Michael's clients always came first, she reminded herself, even at the expense of his family. She could practically guarantee Julie that Michael would be here as soon as he heard what had happened.

"Julie, do you think you can live with the downstairs until Michael comes? He might be able to lift a fingerprint on something, and that could help him trace Johnni."

Julie frowned. "I hate a mess."

Elizabeth glanced at her watch. "I have another hour before I pick up my daughter. I can wait while you grab a toothbrush and pajamas. I insist you come home with us and spend the night."

Julie hesitated for a moment, considering the thought. "I don't want to impose. And I never leave home."

"But don't you see? It would be good for you to get out of this house. You can have a bedroom to yourself, and we won't bother you. It'll just be you and me and Katie."

A little smile touched her lips. "Okay. Just give me a minute."

Elizabeth nodded, glancing once more at the vandalized house. Suddenly she felt the need for some fresh air, and she walked out on the verandah, drinking in the peaceful setting.

This was a lovely estate. How sad to think of the tragedy of Malcomb Waterford, and now the persistent threats of Julie's own sister. Equally frightening was the knowledge that Johnni could invade the house and commit such atrocities.

Elizabeth took a deep breath, absorbing the fresh, clean air. Again, her thoughts circled back to Michael. She had to get him up here; he would know what to do.

In less than ten minutes, Julie came out of the house, locking the door behind her. She looked as though she had washed her face and brushed her hair; she was wearing fresh jeans and a green sweater with ankle boots.

Elizabeth glanced at her watch. "Julie, it'll soon be time for me to pick up Katie at school. Why don't you ride with me? This will be a good chance for you to work on your agoraphobia."

"I don't know…"

"Come on, let's give it a try," she insisted gently. "First, I'm going to grab a tape from my office to put in the tape deck of the car. We can listen to the tape while we ride. It's very soothing; I think it will help you to remain calm. And I'm a good driver," she teased, hoping to relieve the look of concern on Julie's face.

Julie took a shaky breath. "Okay, I'll try," she said, getting in the car with Elizabeth. She said nothing more as they drove along. Elizabeth decided not to try to bridge the silence with useless chatter. Once they pulled up to her front door, she turned to Julie.

"I'll just grab that tape I mentioned."

Julie nodded, saying nothing.

Elizabeth breezed into the house and returned quickly, tape in hand. As she hopped back into the car and pushed the tape into the deck, she smiled at Julie.

"When you overcome agoraphobia, you'll have conquered a major obstacle." Elizabeth started the car again. "The school isn't far," she said, glancing across at Julie, who sat with her hands clenched in her lap, her knuckles white.

"Now just listen to the tape and repeat those phrases in your mind," Elizabeth instructed.

Harp music played in the background. A feminine voice began to speak in a soothing tone: "I am calm...I am in control...."

"Now follow those words in your mind," Elizabeth said, "or say them to yourself while taking deep breaths. It's amazing how deep breathing relaxes the body."

Julie's lips began to move, repeating the words on the tape. Elizabeth could not hear her voice, but she was pleased that at least Julie was trying. And Elizabeth had learned in treating disorders that the longest journey begins with a single step.

Elizabeth said nothing as she guided the car toward the

school. The quiet, two-lane road was canopied with oaks and maples that were beginning to show their fall dress; tinges of red, gold, and orange outlined the road. Elizabeth glanced at Julie. Although her face was pale, she was dutifully following each word on the tape while taking deep breaths in between phrases.

As Elizabeth approached the turnoff to the elementary school, she turned to Julie.

"We'll be meeting other cars, and you'll see children lining up for the school bus, but none of this is a threat to you. You're perfectly safe here in my car."

As they reached the school grounds, Julie's breath was coming in quick gasps. Elizabeth spoke again, trying to emulate the soothing voice on the tape.

"I'll put the gearshift in park and leave the motor running," Elizabeth said calmly. "That way the tape will continue to play while I pick up Katie. All you have to do is listen to the tape, concentrate on the words, and remember nobody is going to say anything to you. You can feel isolated right here in your own world, just as you do at home. Close your eyes if that will help."

Julie nodded, her lips moving in unison with the narrator. *I am calm.... I am in control....*

Saying nothing more, Elizabeth got out of the car and hurried toward the front of the school. She had arrived a few minutes early. As soon as school was dismissed, Katie always waited at the front door for her mother. To save time, Elizabeth dashed down the hall to Katie's room to get her.

Julie sat in the car, her heart beating wildly, her lips moving in unison with the voice on the tape.

"I am calm. I am in control," she spoke aloud, now that

Elizabeth was out of the car. She tried to concentrate on the harp music, on the reassuring words, while continuing with her deep breathing. Her palms were clammy, and she could feel the trickle of perspiration down her neck.

Cars were pulling up in front of the brick school building. A bell pealed out, and she jumped in her seat. Her pulse was racing wildly. She closed her eyes, concentrating on the words, the music....

Julie did not see the car pulling in several cars behind Elizabeth's car. A woman in a black sweatshirt with hood and sunglasses parked at a distance, watching the school. Her head turned as she scanned the parking lot, and the hood slipped back, revealing a flash of red hair.

Thirteen

M ommy, we had a good day," Katie said breathlessly. "Brooke wants me to come over to her house and spend the night. Can I go, please?"

"This is a school night, Katie," Elizabeth informed her as they hurried down the corridor crowded with schoolchildren.

Katie tilted her head back and fixed pleading blue eyes on her mother. "I have straight A's, Mom. You said—"

Her mother laughed softly. "I know what I said. And tonight might be a good night for you to stay with Brooke. We're having an overnight guest, anyway."

Katie's eyes widened hopefully. "Is Dad coming up?"

A sad expression filled her mother's eyes for a moment as she shook her head. She placed her arm around Katie's shoulder as they crossed the parking lot. "No. Mrs. Waterford, our neighbor, is staying."

"Who?" Katie's eyes shot to their car. She could see a woman in the passenger's seat.

"Mrs. Waterford, our neighbor," her mom explained. "So maybe I'll talk with Brooke's mother, and if it's okay with her,

I'll let you go spend the night. But for now, I want you to slip into the backseat and be quiet after I introduce you. Okay?"

Katie was puzzled. Why did her mother use the word *slip?* Mom didn't like people slipping around, and now she was telling Katie to *slip* into the backseat. And why did she want her to be quiet?

Katie's thoughts shot back to Brooke and her invitation to spend the night. They were going to microwave popcorn and watch a video.

"Okay, Mom." She smiled sweetly, doing just as she was told.

Elizabeth opened the door carefully and looked across at Julie. She looked a bit paler, and her breath was heaving in her chest. Elizabeth pretended not to notice.

"We're back and headed home. Katie, this is Mrs. Waterford."

"Hello, Mrs. Waterford." Katie flashed a dimpled smile.

"Hello." Julie nodded at her, then turned back in her seat, staring at the tape.

Elizabeth knew she was concentrating on the words. As she guided the car out of the parking lot, she realized that Julie was trembling slightly. She hoped Katie wouldn't notice and start popping the questions once they were home. If Julie could endure this venture, she would be making real progress.

They had reached the end of the parking lot and were turning onto the two-lane road leading back home.

"Mom, look out!" Katie cried.

Elizabeth swerved, trying to get out of the path of the car that zipped past them. She regained control of the wheel, and now it was Elizabeth's turn to take a deep breath.

"That lady shouldn't be driving so fast in a school zone, should she, Mom?"

Elizabeth swallowed and tried to find her voice, and calm it in the process, but it was difficult. "No, darling, she shouldn't. And she went by so fast I didn't see who was with her. Probably some kids eager to get home for after-school treats," she said, hoping to reassure both Katie and Julie, while getting a grip herself.

She had to be more careful; she was driving too fast. But she was anxious to get out of the crowd and back home. She hadn't even seen the car come up behind them.

Her eyes darted to Julie. She had leaned her head back against the seat; her eyes were closed, her body visibly trembling.

Suddenly, the car was quiet again, with only the sound of the tape. "I am calm.... I am in control...."

Fourteen

Michael had thoroughly enjoyed the small group of Promise Keepers, and being with Jay had lifted his spirits. As he unlocked the door and entered his town house, a feeling of peace settled over him. He felt less lonely than usual upon coming home. Again, he reviewed the meeting. He was amazed at the way men hugged and seemed genuinely concerned with one another's problems. He recalled the testimony he had heard from one guy in particular, a guy who had been separated from his family but was now back with them, happy again. Of course, Jay had known in advance about the speaker, and that was why he had called Michael.

Sly fox, he thought, grinning. Though he had seen through Jay's motives, Michael had listened intently to the principles on which Promise Keepers was founded. One promise, in particular, seemed to speak to him. Each man had emphasized the importance of family time, and Michael knew, with a sinking heart, that he had failed in that department. He thought of Katie and Elizabeth with deep sadness. He had cheated their little family out of valuable memories all those times he had chosen to work late instead of coming home. He was even late for Katie's last birthday party. Elizabeth had found this inexcusable—and she was justified in her feelings. Katie was more forgiving, particularly after he slipped her a twenty-dollar bill.

But the guys he met at Promise Keepers emphasized that it was never too late to start making up for lost time with one's family. What also impressed Michael was the way these men allowed themselves to be open and vulnerable. He had brought this up with Jay on the way home.

"I guess I'm stuck in the macho groove," Michael confessed to Jay. "Wanting to be strong and tough."

"You can still be strong and tough." Jay glanced from the traffic to Michael. "Just apply that strength to keeping the principles of Promise Keepers. I'm a better Christian as a result, Michael, and I know that being a Promise Keeper has strengthened my marriage."

Michael took a deep breath, trying to absorb those words. He tapped Jay's shoulder.

"Hey, I'm glad you and Tracy are so happy."

Jay grinned. "Our marriage is great, and for two strong-willed, career-oriented people, that's saying a lot."

He reached into the backseat and retrieved a book. "Here, take this. It's one of the books written for Promise Keepers. Put it on your bedside table, and read it when you get a chance. It'll help you," Jay added gently.

Flipping through the book as he entered his living room, Michael was lost in thought. For a couple of minutes he didn't notice the red light blinking on his answering machine. Then it caught his eye, and he walked over to scan his Caller ID. Two calls from the office, two unavailables, and then one from Elizabeth.

Quickly, he ran through the messages on the answering machine. The office calls had been from Anita, asking him to please call Elizabeth as soon as possible. He waited impatiently until Elizabeth's voice came on the machine.

"Michael, could you please call me as soon as you come in? It's about Julie Waterford and it's terribly important."

He frowned, going to the next message. It was from Tommy.

"Hi, Michael. I spent some time checking out Buckhead with the sketch of Johnni. Nothing yet, but I'll keep trying."

Feeling anxious, he dialed the phone number at Oak Shadows.

It rang four times, and he was about to hang up when Elizabeth's voice came over the wire.

"Am I calling too late?" he asked.

"No, I was waiting on your call. Michael, can you come up in the morning?" She sounded upset. "Johnni came to Julie's house while she was out and wrecked the place. Julie's spending the night here, to avoid the mess. I told her not to touch anything until you could look around." She lowered her voice. "It's absolutely horrible. Julie's painting is slashed, the living room is a mess, and she's thrown Julie's clothes around the bedroom. And she initialed a *J* in vivid purple lipstick on Julie's bathroom mirror. We're dealing with a very sick woman."

Michael listened, astounded by what he was hearing. He raked through his hair, trying to remember his schedule. It didn't matter; he had finished with the court case, and everything else could go on hold. "Tell Julie I'll be there around nine in the morning. Incidentally, I've hired a guy part-time to do nothing but show a copy of Julie's picture—the one the sketch artist improvised, changing the hair and eyes. We already have a lead on Johnni."

"That's a relief." He heard her sigh.

Michael hesitated, making a quick decision as his thoughts returned to the meeting of Promise Keepers. "And, Elizabeth...I'd like to take Katie fishing if you don't mind."

There was a pause. "When?"

"While I'm up there tomorrow. I thought maybe Katie could check out of school early if it's not a problem. I wanted to take her fishing for a couple of hours before I have to come back to Atlanta."

Several seconds of silence followed, as he found himself thinking of those times, years ago, when he had taken both Katie and Elizabeth to the lake to picnic and fish. He wasn't sure if the silence on the other end of the wire meant Elizabeth was remembering, too, or if she was thinking of a tactful way to refuse.

"I think that would be great, Michael," she finally responded. "And there's a lake not far from here."

"Good. If she has something at school, we can reschedule it. I just thought I would offer. It will only take a couple of hours."

"No problem, she's making straight A's. I think it's important for her to go fishing with you. She always loved that."

"Good," he said, trying to sound more matter-of-fact. "I'll go to Julie's house, then come on over."

"Thanks, Michael," Elizabeth said. "I'll check her out of school early. She's spending the night with Brooke, but I won't call this late. I'll just pick her up at school in the morning. She'll be thrilled to go fishing with you."

Was there more tenderness to her tone, or was he imagining it, hoping for it? Either way, he felt good about the prospect of spending time with Katie.

Fifteen

With Katie out of the house, Elizabeth and Julie had spent a quiet evening. Julie had brought along a best-seller she had been wanting to read, and she retired to the guest bedroom early. Elizabeth had worked in her office until Michael called, then gone up to bed.

She was sleeping soundly, at last, when suddenly a thud echoed through the house. Instantly awake, Elizabeth turned on the bedside lamp. She sat up in bed, listening.

Trying to ignore the fear that raced through her, she jumped out of bed, slipped her housecoat on over her pajamas, and shoved her feet into slippers.

She looked to her bedroom window. She could see the branches of the oak tree flailing against the wind. Perhaps that was what had awakened her. The wind in the trees. No...

There was that sound again. What was it? A board creaking? A door opening?

Shaking her hair back from her face, she crept toward her closed door and gently turned the knob.

In the hallway, all was quiet. She hesitated, glancing down

to the end of the hall, to the guest bedroom where Julie was sleeping. There was silence. The noise must have come from downstairs.

The hall night-light she kept burning for Katie and herself cast a dim glow down the circular stairs; still, there were pockets of shadows along the way. She hesitated at the top of the stairs, listening. There was no sound other than the wind blowing through the trees.

Gripping the banister, she descended the stairs to look around. She recalled the words on the tape she had played for Julie.

I am calm. I am in control, she told herself.

As was her custom, she had left a few lights on downstairs, and now she crept from one room to another, inspecting everything. Somewhere in the distance, she could hear a board creaking, the sound an odd, yet familiar, rhythm. What was it?

Nothing was out of place in any of the rooms. Everything seemed normal. Still, she could hear the distant rhythm.

As she crossed her office she peered through the window to the verandah. The wind was whipping across the front porch. A rocking chair was moving gently, back and forth, back and forth, as though a demon spirit were sitting there, enjoying the storm.

She heaved a sigh of relief. The creak of the rocker—that's all she had heard.

Relieved, she turned to start back up the steps, but this time there was no mistaking another sound: a woman's cry.

She yanked up the long skirt of her housecoat and raced up the winding stairs, her eyes lifted up toward the upper hallway.

"Julie?" she called, almost stumbling halfway up the stairs, then catching herself on the railing. She forced herself to take a deep, long breath and continue upward, certain now that the sounds she had been hearing were coming from the guest bedroom.

She flew down the hall and turned the knob on the door. The lamp was burning on the nightstand. The covers were thrown back, the bed empty.

"Julie?" she called, trying not to identify the unnamed fear that brought a bitter taste to her mouth. The room was cold, and she could see why: The door to the verandah was half open.

Cautiously, she approached the door, opening it wider.

Julie was leaning against the wooden balcony, staring down into the darkness as the wind whipped her white chiffon gown around her slender body.

"Julie! What are you doing out here?" Elizabeth cried, rushing out onto the balcony.

The glow from the bedroom light cast a pale tint to Julie's face; Elizabeth could see the terror etched on Julie's features. Her brown eyes seemed dazed as she stared at Elizabeth.

"It's freezing out here, Julie," Elizabeth said gently, taking her cold hand. "Come back inside."

She followed Elizabeth like a child lost in the dark. Elizabeth found herself thinking of Malcomb Waterford, wondering what kind of woman she had been when he married her. And what he would do for her now, if he could see what had become of her.

Once inside, Elizabeth closed the door and reached for Julie's white satin robe, which was tossed over the back of a chair. She draped the robe around Julie's trembling body as Julie pressed a hand to her right temple.

"The nightmares!" Julie said in a weak voice. "They're driving me crazy. Afterwards, it's as though Johnni's in the room with me."

"But she isn't," Elizabeth said firmly.

"Just before I wake up, I hear her whispering to me about our childhood, about Malcomb."

Elizabeth took a deep breath, trying to dispel the fear and concern that had rushed through her. Her first thought was hot cocoa.

"Do you know my remedy for bad dreams?" she asked with a smile.

Julie turned lost eyes to her. "What?"

"I go down to the kitchen, make hot cocoa, and sit at the table till my head clears. Let's do that now."

Julie nodded vaguely. "Okay."

As they sat at the kitchen table, sipping hot cocoa, Julie seemed to have recovered from her nightmare. In fact, it was she, not Elizabeth, who was doing the talking.

"I think Johnni has been sneaking around for years," she said, sipping the warm cocoa that Elizabeth had poured into large white mugs.

"Why do you say that?" Elizabeth frowned. What was that supposed to mean?

"On my sixteenth birthday, my parents gave me a white convertible. I loved it. One day I came out of school, and the door was bashed in."

"Maybe someone backed into you and didn't report it," Elizabeth suggested.

"Maybe. But there was no paint on the door."

The wind moaned outside the kitchen window, and Elizabeth got up to refill their cups.

"And then there was the accident."

Elizabeth returned to the table with more hot cocoa.

"What accident?"

"Malcomb's accident. *Our* accident."

"Do you want to talk about what happened?" Elizabeth asked gently.

116

Julie took a deep breath, staring down into her cup. "Malcomb and I were returning from Atlanta. He was recovering from a bout of influenza. I was driving. We had left the interstate and were on the two-lane, about ten miles from here. A logging truck had wrecked; there were logs all over the highway...."

Elizabeth leaned forward in her seat, her elbows propped on the table, her hands cradling her mug of cocoa. "Then what happened?"

Julie shook her head, blinking rapidly as she related the accident. "I swerved to miss a log and ended up in the oncoming lane. A car hit us.... The car never stopped. Later, Malcomb died from injuries sustained in our wreck." She placed her mug carefully on the table and gripped her hands tightly. "After that, I started to have the nightmares."

"Tell me about the first one."

Julie closed her eyes. "I'm running from Bull. I have to escape...."

"Sometimes our nightmares are based on fears. You were reliving a fear, Julie."

She nodded. "I guess so."

Elizabeth looked across the table at her. Julie seemed so frail, so vulnerable. It was inhumane what her twin sister was doing to her, after all Julie had already endured.

"Julie, I want to help you feel safe again. Safe from the nightmares. Safe from Johnni."

Julie took a deep breath and finished her cocoa. "Oh, how I want to feel that way again," she said. "With Malcomb, I always felt safe. That's one reason his death has been so hard for me." Tilting her head to the right, she smiled across at Elizabeth. "You know, you're really a good person. I appreciate your help."

"There's someone who can give you far greater help than I can, or even Malcomb—"

"You're talking about God, aren't you?" Julie said, a defensive edge to her tone.

"Yes, I am. You know, he's the only real security we have. Since you managed to get through the school traffic today, I was wondering if you would be interested in joining my small-group Bible study each week. There are only a few of us, but we meet at different homes, and we pray for one another. I think it would be helpful to you, Julie."

Julie was quiet for several seconds, tracing the rim of her mug with a small finger. "I'll think about it," she said quietly.

"Good," Elizabeth said, taking a deep breath. "Now, what do you say we call it a night."

"Can I help you rinse out the cups or something?"

"Nope, just hop in bed."

As Julie left the room, Elizabeth took the mugs and spoons to the sink and stood for a moment looking out into the angry night. The wind had died down now, but the rain had started to fall in heavy sheets.

She thought of Katie and Brooke, probably whispering long after lights were out. She had called earlier to check on her, and Brooke's mom reported that the girls were nestled in Brooke's bedroom, watching a video on her small pink television set and VCR.

As she washed and dried the cups, Elizabeth glanced at the wall phone in the kitchen. She felt a strong urge to call Michael just to hear his voice. When Julie had mentioned feeling safe with Malcomb, Elizabeth had identified with those words. Her mother had always chastised Elizabeth for being too independent for her own good—and maybe she was. Yet she had appreciated Michael's strength and had cherished the contentment she felt when wrapped in his loving arms. She had known a sense of completion in being a wife and mother. Before the problems began...

She was not going to let her thoughts stray further, she told herself as she put the cups away and turned out the kitchen light.

Sixteen

Friday, October 4

Michael had left Atlanta early, grabbing coffee and a sausage and biscuit at a drive-through near his town house. Sipping and munching, he arrived at Julie Waterford's house around nine, as promised. When he pulled to a stop in the driveway, he spotted Julie seated on the porch, dressed in jeans and a black turtleneck.

She stood as he got out of the car and gave him a half-smile. As he approached her, he decided she looked much better than he expected, after his conversation with Elizabeth.

"Elizabeth told me what happened. May I come in?"

"Sure. I spent the night at Elizabeth's house last night. I just got here. I've unlocked the door, but I didn't want to go inside. It felt good just sitting here in the sunshine."

"Yeah, it's a nice fall morning. I'm working on finding your sister," Michael said, climbing the porch steps, "but there's no Johnni Hankins with a driver's license, car registration, or voting record. She must be going by a married name."

Lucifer rounded a corner, arching his back and hissing at Michael, who could only shake his head.

"He looks like a good pet for your sister," he mumbled under his breath, but Julie was opening the door and hadn't heard him. Or she had chosen to ignore his sarcasm.

"I left everything downstairs just the way I found it." She led the way into the foyer and waited while Michael looked around. He agreed with Elizabeth: They had a sick woman on their hands.

Books were tumbled from bookshelves. The glass on Malcomb Waterford's portrait had been smashed. The portrait itself was untouched. Cigarette butts with vivid purple lipstick overflowed the ashtray.

"What else did she do?"

"Upstairs…" Julie led the way up the circular staircase to the bedroom, where Michael came up short. It was a horrible mess, clothes strewn everywhere. The vivid purple *J* on the bathroom mirror was particularly significant, he decided.

He turned back to Julie. "What's she trying to prove?"

"That she's been here. And that I don't deserve any of the nice things I have now."

Michael arched an eyebrow. "You think that's all it is?"

Julie shrugged. "She didn't really steal anything," she said, almost defensively. "All she took was a couple of nice dresses. I never go out anymore. It doesn't matter. I would have given them to her if only she had asked. It's just that…" Her voice trailed off as she turned wide brown eyes to Michael. "I wish I could make her stop hating me."

Michael indicated the door. "Let's go back downstairs."

He stared after her as she led the way back downstairs. Julie looked so small and frail, and he felt all his protective instincts rush forth. He touched her shoulder gently. "We'll find her. Then we'll get some professional help."

"Elizabeth, you mean?"

He smiled, sensing Julie's respect for Elizabeth. "Elizabeth definitely will help."

For the first time a vague smile touched her pale lips. "Your wife's a wonderful woman. It makes me feel better just talking to her."

He stared at Julie for a moment. This was the first time he had actually spoken with one of Elizabeth's clients. It was touching to realize that she really did help people like Julie, who was obviously a sweet person.

"I'm glad you feel that way about her," he said, turning back to survey the damage. His eyes lingered on the ashtray.

"This isn't your lipstick, is it?"

Julie shook her head. "I don't even smoke."

"Julie, do you have a Ziploc bag I could use?" he asked.

"What are you going to do?"

"Start tracking her."

Julie looked slightly bewildered by those words as she turned toward the kitchen.

Meanwhile, Michael started to pick up tumbled books. He was surprised to see a book of Psalms on the floor. Gently, he picked it up and opened the cover. Elizabeth's name, in her own handwriting, was inscribed across the inside page. Tenderness swelled in his heart as he thought of Elizabeth trying to help this poor woman, helping her in the best possible way—by giving her God's Word. And this woman needed that kind of comfort, now more than ever.

He needed to survey the outside. "I'd like to look over your property, if you don't mind," he called to her.

"Go ahead," Julie replied from the kitchen.

Once outside, he made a quick search of the grounds around the house. An enclosed double garage with a gray Mercedes parked inside connected to the left side of the house.

To the right, a white fence enclosed a patio, pool, and pool house. He was glad Katie didn't know about the pool. The way she loved to swim, she'd jump at the chance to splash around in that pool on a warm day. But he really didn't want her over here until this case was settled.

Michael walked around the lounge chairs near the pool and glanced at the blue water sparkling in the sunshine. He peered inside the pool house.

A cozy sitting room with yellow walls and white wicker furnishings adjoined a small dressing room and bath.

He walked back out and looked beyond the fence. The meadow stretched to the woods where he had seen the doe come out.

Turning, he retraced his steps back to the house, crossing the side lawn to the front of the house.

"You asked for a Ziploc bag with the cigarette butts," Julie said.

He looked down. She had neatly deposited them within the bag, and he mentally scolded himself for not doing that. Now her fingerprints would be on the cigarette butts, possibly smudging Johnni's. Still, there was a good chance they could lift a print and track Johnni. Maybe she had a police record.

"Thanks," he said, accepting the plastic bag. "Incidentally, I'm already making progress on finding her."

"How?" She tilted her head to one side and studied him curiously.

"I've located someone who has seen her."

"You have?" Julie asked incredulously.

He nodded, trying to force a reassuring smile as he looked down at Julie. "Try not to worry. We'll find her. Now I gotta run." He hesitated before leaving. "Sure you'll be okay?"

She nodded, but something in her expression lacked conviction.

"Don't hesitate to call me or Elizabeth if you need us."

"Thanks," she said, looking sad again as she watched him leave.

By the time he reached Elizabeth's house, his concern had escalated. He picked up his mobile phone and called the office. As soon as Anita answered, he began to speak.

"Anita, please find Tommy Kline's number on the Rolodex in my office and see if you can reach him. Tell him we have a break in the Johnni case. I'll be back in Atlanta somewhere around seven or seven-thirty. Maybe I could meet him for dinner, before or after his class."

Anita replied with her usual efficiency and then said goodbye. He glanced at the Ziploc bag, his thoughts racing. He already knew what he wanted Tommy to do. He spun into Elizabeth's drive, then forced himself to slow down. The old eagerness to get right on a case tugged at him, but this time he was not going to break a promise to his daughter. They were going fishing for a couple of hours.

As he neared the house, he spotted Katie and Elizabeth sitting in the rockers on the porch, rocking and talking. He smiled. Just the sight of them warmed his heart.

When he stopped the Jeep and got out, Katie raced to meet him. She was already dressed for their little fishing trip—old jeans and sweatshirt, an Atlanta Braves baseball cap snug on her blonde head.

"Daddy!" Her blue eyes glowed beneath the bib of the cap as she tilted her head up at him, and his heart melted. "Mom picked me up early at school. She told my teacher it was a special appointment, but she didn't say what." A gleam of intrigue lit her blue eyes. "After we left school, she told me that you and I are going fishing."

"Yeah, maybe we'll catch a big one."

Elizabeth was watching them from the porch. "Hop in the car," he said to Katie.

As he approached Elizabeth, she met him at the steps. "I've just left Julie Waterford's house." He lowered his voice. "We've got a real lulu on our hands with that Johnni. I'll get back on it the minute I hit town this afternoon."

She nodded, her eyes drifting toward Katie, who was settling into the car. "But you're still taking Katie fishing."

"I promised," he said simply.

Their eyes locked, and for one insane moment, he wanted to take her in his arms, kiss her passionately, and have her respond as she once did. But Katie was blowing the horn.

Pulling his eyes from Elizabeth, he glanced at his watch. He knew exactly what time it was. He merely wanted to break the spell.

He glanced back and caught her taking a deep breath. Was she feeling a mix of emotions as well?

"We'll only be gone a couple of hours. I'll talk with you more about Julie when I return. I don't think Johnni will be back tonight."

"Neither do I," Elizabeth agreed. "There's a public lake and picnic site just this side of Springville. You turn right at that bait shop, and the lake is straight out the road about half a mile or so."

He nodded. "Thanks. That's the lake I had in mind, but I wasn't sure about the exact location. Well, see you later." He hurried back to the car, fighting the impulse to invite Elizabeth to go with them.

When he got in the Jeep, Katie was frowning at the Ziploc bag of cigarette butts. She looked accusingly at him but asked nothing. *Wise kid*, he thought wryly. "Mrs. Waterford, your neighbor, was visited by a very mean sister. We're trying to locate her. I'm taking those to a lab for fingerprints."

"Yuk, what an ugly color of lipstick. Mom would never wear anything like that."

He smiled. "I know." He opened the glove compartment and placed the bag inside. "In fact, we'll use that shade of lipstick to help track her down."

"Are we gonna hook a big one today, Dad?" Katie asked, bored with the subject of his work.

He winked at her. "Maybe. Here, let's buckle up." He reached over to buckle her seat belt, then impulsively leaned down to plant a kiss on her cheek. She didn't deserve the mess her parents were in. They had to patch things up somehow. The message he had gotten from Promise Keepers gave him new hope.

"Did you bring my fishing pole?" Katie inquired. "We haven't been fishing in a long time, have we?"

"No, we haven't," he admitted, feeling a mixture of guilt and regret. "And yes, I brought your fishing pole. Maybe we can start fishing again more often."

"Great!"

Michael turned the key in the ignition, glancing back at the three-story mansion with its chipped paint and sagging green shutters. Elizabeth had already gone back inside.

He sighed heavily. He still couldn't fathom why she had been so persistent about living out here. As they drove off, however, his eyes roamed the tranquil setting, and reluctantly he found himself absorbing the peace and quiet. It was a welcome reprieve after dealing with traffic and interstates in the city. The air held a fresh sweetness, and the big oaks were beginning to turn. It would be gorgeous here in a few weeks.

The problem was, he hated Oak Shadows. Or was it really the blue blood money he hated? *Come on, Calloway, tell the truth*, his conscience nagged. He was a poor farm boy who had scraped his way up the ladder to earn a name for himself as one of Atlanta's most successful businessmen. And he had done it through grueling work and fierce determination. Oak Shadows had been handed to Elizabeth on a silver platter, like so many other things. One of them had to give in, grow up. And neither seemed ready.

"Where are we going fishing?" Katie asked, her mind jumping ahead to the time they would spend together.

"Not too far from here. How was school today?"

"Fine." She smiled at her father. "I want you to meet my friend, Brooke."

Michael nodded. "Okay. Maybe we can take her fishing with us next time."

"That'd be neat." Katie flashed him a wide grin.

He glanced at his daughter, so full of innocence, so protected from the ugliness of the world. He hated for her to grow up, to be exposed to the sick minds out there. This was another reason he had chosen his profession well, he assured himself. He worked daily to lessen the dangers for good citizens.

"How's school going?" he asked Katie, wanting to clear his mind.

She began her usual chatter, and he nodded at the appropriate times as he drove along. The mess he had seen inside the Waterford house continued to haunt him, but he tried to clear his head of everything related to work. He was determined to devote the next couple of hours to Katie. Then when he returned to Atlanta, his search for Johnni would go into overdrive.

He found the turnoff to the lake and wound down the road past the park, stopping the car in the shade of an oak tree. He reached into the backseat for their fishing poles.

"Have you forgotten what I taught you?" He glanced at Katie.

"Dad! I know how to fish," she protested, her pride obviously injured by his question.

Michael smiled. He had no doubt that she remembered what he had taught her, for she was quick to learn. He and

Elizabeth had been blessed with a child who could be given instructions once, rarely twice, and then proceed to follow those instructions with ease.

They spent more than an hour in the late morning sun, catching only a few small catfish and releasing them. Michael's habit was to catch and release, unless he was fishing for food, and this time there was no need for that. He and his daughter were merely here to have fun. He must remember to call Jay and thank him for that invitation to Promise Keepers. The message he had received from those guys had led him to make a date with his daughter...and to keep it this time!

After a few hours of fishing and a stop-off at a restaurant that specialized in hamburgers, they headed back to Oak Shadows.

"Dad..."

"Yeah, Katie, what is it?"

"Mom still keeps that picture of us by her bed. Sometimes she cries when she looks at it."

Michael felt his throat tighten at those words. "And sometimes I cry, too, Katie."

"Oh, Dad! You never cry." She tilted her blue eyes up to him, unbelieving.

"Katie—" he pulled her closer to him—"there's nothing wrong with a man crying when it hurts. I never taught you that, did I? Well, we're learning together, pal."

Seventeen

L ater, as they drove past the Waterford Farm sign, Katie turned in her seat and stared up the drive.

"Dad, what's wrong with Mrs. Waterford?" she asked suddenly. Michael was so deep in thought about their own situation that it took him a few seconds to catch up with Katie's change of subject.

He followed her eyes up the driveway, considering the question she had asked. What was wrong? Michael wasn't sure. "Your mother could answer that better than I. But basically, she's troubled about a jealous twin sister, and my job is to find the sister. Your mother's job is to help Mrs. Waterford get over all the troubles that she's experienced."

Katie nodded, as though satisfied with that explanation. Then, after a thoughtful silence, she tilted her blonde head back and fastened those engaging blue eyes upon her father again. "You and Mom both have important jobs, don't you?"

He nodded, taking a deep, long breath. "Yes, we do, Katie." It was the first time he had given Elizabeth the credit she deserved. He was ashamed of himself for being so stubborn.

When they arrived back at Elizabeth's house, Michael felt a reluctance to leave.

"I have to tell your mother something," he said, following Katie up the steps to the front door.

As they entered the foyer, Katie swung around to give Michael a kiss. "Dad, thanks for taking me fishing this afternoon."

He reached out, tweaking her cheek. "My pleasure." He glanced up and saw Elizabeth standing in the doorway to a room that obviously was used as her office now. He could see her desk and chair, bookshelves, and the array of green plants that she had always said brought tranquillity to her office.

"I don't have much time, but I need to talk with you about Julie Waterford." He glanced over his shoulder, waiting until Katie had dashed up the stairs.

Elizabeth motioned Michael into her office. He entered and she took a seat behind her desk. He dropped down in the Queen Anne chair that faced her.

"Is this where your clients sit?" he asked.

She nodded, her eyes watching him carefully.

He nodded, running his arms up and down the armrest. "I was just trying to imagine timid little Julie sitting here, voicing her frustrations. I feel sorry for that woman," he said, looking from the brocade of the chair to Elizabeth's thoughtful gaze.

"So do I. Do you think you can find Johnni?"

"I have to. We have a very sick woman on the loose. When I get back to Atlanta, I'm meeting with Tommy Kline, the guy I hired to help on the case. We'll accelerate the search even more. In fact, it has top priority now." He glanced at his watch. "I can just make the lab if I hurry back to town. I'm going to have those cigarette butts checked out."

Elizabeth nodded. "Then what do you plan to do?" she asked, leaning forward in her chair, watching him intently.

"You know the sketch I had made of Johnni? I've already learned that she resembles the picture except for the hairdo, which I'll have Chuck revise first thing tomorrow."

"Oh? How?" Elizabeth was fascinated.

"A hostess at the Sun Dial lounge at the Peachtree is pretty sure that's the woman who's been coming in. Chuck gave her a short hairdo, but we were slightly off. She wears it in a kind of shag."

Elizabeth nodded thoughtfully. "That's a popular style now."

"The hostess promised to call me if she comes back. But I have to do more," he said, crossing his legs at his ankles, staring thoughtfully at his Reeboks.

"Sounds as though you're already doing a lot," Elizabeth acknowledged, a different tone in her voice. Then she leaned forward, a frown marring her smooth brow. "Michael, you know what nags at me about this situation? Dr. Waterford's accident. That keeps cropping up in the back of my mind."

Michael frowned at her, trying to follow her train of thought.

"What do you mean?"

"This so-called accident that Johnni has threatened on Julie before their next birthday. I keep thinking about the car wreck that took Dr. Waterford's life. Do you suppose there's any connection to Johnni's weird stuff and Dr. Waterford's accident? Another car was involved in the wreck, but that driver was never located."

Michael chewed the inside corner of his lip, thinking about the implications. "I can see why that bothers you. I'll look into it. Try to find out more about that accident in your next conversation with Julie."

She nodded. "I will. Michael, thanks for your help."

"You're welcome." Michael studied Elizabeth's face. There was something different in her eyes. He couldn't analyze what she was thinking. He shifted uncomfortably in the chair and glanced at his watch. "I'd better go."

He wondered, later, why Elizabeth had noticeably tensed at those words. He couldn't figure out what she expected of him, but then there were mysteries about Elizabeth that he was yet to understand, even after ten years of marriage.

"Thanks for taking Katie," she said, remaining seated. She was obviously not seeing him to the door.

What a contrast to their good-byes in the past! Elizabeth always used to follow him to the door, kiss him good-bye. She obviously didn't feel that way anymore. Something inside him turned cold again.

"We had fun fishing," he said matter-of-factly, turning to walk out of her office. "Bye, Katie," he called up the stairs. Then he hurried through the door, down the steps, away from the house. Away from Elizabeth and a marriage that seemed filled with conflict. As he started the Jeep and drove away, he realized the wedge between them had widened again, just when he thought he was making progress.

Elizabeth sat at the desk for a long time, listening to the engine of Michael's Jeep fade into the afternoon. She was touched by the time he had spent with Katie, and she was grateful that he was giving Julie's case top priority.

So what is wrong? She dragged herself out of the chair, forcing her feet in the direction of the kitchen. She had never liked cooking. When they were in the city, she had become spoiled by convenience stores, drive-through eateries, and nice restaurants. But cooking was part of the price she paid for living at Oak Shadows.

Something nagged at her, and she knew what it was: the feelings she still had for Michael. The anger and resentment that had propelled her from him a month ago were melting away. Maybe she had judged him too harshly. Christians were expected to forgive, but she had been unable to do that for a while. Now, it seemed to her, she was beginning to change; she sensed that he was, as well.

Still, one fishing trip didn't make up to Katie for all the other times he had neglected both of them for his work. She might feel more forgiving, but rushing back into his arms was another matter. There would have to be a wait-and-see period. The heated arguments returned to her mind, reinforcing the need for a cooling-off period. The problem was, she was tempted to skip that part and feel the comfort of his strong arms, as Katie had today.

It would be so easy to give in, return to the city, relinquish her commitment to this place. But she couldn't do that. She had made a promise to herself, to Grandmother, as well, and maybe to all her ancestors. She had to hold on for a while longer.

Opening a cabinet, she surveyed the canned goods, remembering that Katie liked chili.

"Canned chili it is," she said with relief, removing a couple of cans, then rummaging around for a can opener.

As she opened the cans, her eyes drifted into space, and she found herself recalling a candlelight dinner she had shared with Michael a few years back. It had been a special occasion: Valentine's Day. Michael had brought her roses, her favorite; then he took her to a special Italian restaurant and proposed to her all over again. They laughed together and stayed out past the baby-sitter's hour, behaving as recklessly as teenagers. But it was so much fun. And later that evening, they went to their bedroom, hand in hand, where they shared a sweet, passionate evening together.

The next morning, Michael served Elizabeth breakfast in

bed, with a single rose from the bouquet lying beside her plate on the tray.

Tears pooled in her eyes as she stared at the can in her hand.

"Oh, Michael," she whispered sadly, "I miss you so much. I miss *us*."

Admitting it made her feel a tiny bit better, but it did nothing to lessen the pain in her heart.

Michael arrived at Stallworth Laboratories just as it was closing.

"It'll only take a minute," he informed a frowning doorman as he pushed past to catch up with Yeong, who was removing his white lab jacket. Upon seeing Michael, the young man began to groan.

"Come on, Yeong. This is an easy one."

"How easy?" he asked doubtfully.

Michael removed the Ziploc bag of cigarette butts from his pocket. "I'll only leave a few."

Shaking his head, Yeong walked back to his desk to remove a plastic bag. Michael shook several butts from one bag to the other.

"There'll be more than one set of prints on there. Just get both."

"Is the lady missing or is she a murderer?" Yeong asked, staring at the lipstick.

"Missing. Murder may be next. So you see, Yeong, I need you. When can I expect a phone call?"

"Couple of days. My assistant just had a baby."

"But, Yeong, that perfect steak at the Highland Tap—remember?"

"I must also remember those in line before you."

"Touché." Michael grinned. "I'll be waiting."

Eighteen

From the laboratory, Michael made a dash home to change clothes and check his messages.

When he returned Tommy's call, they agreed to meet at nine, after Tommy's last class.

"You name the place," Michael suggested.

"How about Lulu's? It's one of my favorite hangouts."

"Fine with me. See you then."

Later, as Michael parked his Jeep in the crowded parking lot, he reached into the glove compartment and removed the Ziploc bag containing the lipstick-stained cigarette butts. He tucked the bag into the pocket of his jeans and got out, locking the Jeep. Walking toward the restaurant, he noticed the mural featuring deer, crawfish, catfish, and an alligator. He rubbed his stomach, aware for the first time of how hungry he was.

Once inside, he peered across the crowd until he spotted Tommy waving him to a seat. He hurried across the room.

"Glad you didn't wait on me." He grinned at Tommy's plate, which was already filled.

"Man, I didn't even get lunch. Try the catfish; it's terrific."

"Sounds good," he said as a server approached.

"I'll have an order exactly like his." He noted Tommy's soft drink. "The only exception is, I'd like sweetened tea with a thick slice of lemon."

"Coming right up," the server promised, dashing toward the kitchen.

"What's up?" Tommy asked, pouring more ketchup onto his plate.

"Johnni came back to Mrs. Waterford's house and left her signature. We've got to find her soon. This is a dangerous woman."

"A beautiful…dangerous…woman." Tommy shook his head.

"Don't be deceived. I think she's smart as well as dangerous, so be careful," Michael warned.

The server dashed up with a plate of hot food, and Michael thanked him and started to eat. Then he remembered something. He reached into his pocket and removed the Ziploc bag of purple-stained cigarette butts.

Tommy's eyes widened. Then he glanced self-consciously around the room before leaning toward Michael and lowering his voice. "What am I supposed to do with those?"

"I want you to visit the cosmetic sections of some department stores around town."

Tommy's mouth fell open. "How many stores?"

Michael grinned. "Don't panic. Just the ones in Lennox Mall and Cumberland Mall, for starters. Look for this shade of lipstick, and then the ladies who buy it. Maybe Johnni used a credit card. That'll give us an address."

Tommy was staring at the cigarette butts. "Unusual color."

"Yep, and that's a break for us. You still have the picture of her?"

Tommy nodded. "It's in my car."

"Show her picture to the salesclerks. Be creative with your reason for finding her. And remember, we have to find her before next Friday. That gives us a week."

"Lucky thing I've got the weekend coming up, and I'm not overloaded with homework, for a change." He frowned. "But just out of curiosity, what happens in a week?"

Michael sighed, reaching for his tea. "Next Friday happens to be Julie and Johnni's birthday. Johnni has threatened an accident about that time. From what I've seen, I have no doubt she'll attempt to pull one off. Julie's in danger."

Tommy looked around self-consciously before shoving the Ziploc bag in his pocket.

"Maybe one of us will get lucky," Tommy said, but the frown on his face revealed his doubt.

Michael sighed. "Yeah, a little luck and a lot of old-fashioned detective work are what we need."

Nineteen

E lizabeth phoned Julie after she and Katie had finished their chili.

"Julie, it's Elizabeth. I just wanted to be sure that everything is okay."

"Elizabeth, I've been thinking. Maybe Johnni was just trying to upset me." Over the wire, Julie's voice sounded calmer, more relaxed. Elizabeth breathed a sigh of relief. "Maybe now that she has her revenge, that's all she wants. I don't want you and Michael worrying about me."

Elizabeth hesitated, choosing her words carefully. "We care about you, Julie. So if we worry, that's why."

"Maybe she won't bother me anymore."

Elizabeth closed her eyes, wishing this were true, but she doubted it. In fact, she was more concerned than ever about Johnni.

"I hope you're right. Still, I think you should be cautious. Always check your Caller ID before you answer the phone. If you can get a number on her, call me right away. Michael can work with a telephone number."

"I will."

Elizabeth pursed her lips. "You said your Caller ID shows *unavailable* when she calls. There's a code the caller can use to block the number from showing up. I learned that from Michael. Would you object to having your line tapped? It may come to that, you know."

When Julie hesitated, Elizabeth felt she should not press her to do anything she didn't want to do.

"We'll just see what happens," Elizabeth continued smoothly. "I want you to know that I'll be here all weekend. I have no plans, so if you want to drop by, feel free to do so. If you get worried or frightened, just come on over. Katie and I will be glad to have you here. My only plans are a meeting with an interior decorator in the morning."

"You're starting on your renovation?"

Elizabeth took a deep breath. "Depends on what she tells me. She's driving up from Atlanta, and I trust her judgment. If she tells me I'm in over my head, I'll take it as the gospel."

"Does that mean you would move back to Atlanta?"

"I doubt that I'd give up that easily, after all. But I do want to know the extent of what I might be getting into before I start."

"Sounds like a good idea." She paused for a moment. "I was fortunate that this house was already renovated when I married Malcomb. He was married once before, you know."

Elizabeth couldn't remember if she had known that or not. "What happened with the first marriage, may I ask? Or would you rather not say?"

"I think she grew tired of Malcomb's devotion to his work. He was a brilliant man, you know. And I'm glad he was devoted to his teaching; otherwise, I wouldn't have met him."

"You were in one of his classes?" Elizabeth hoped she wasn't prying, but she had wondered how the two got together.

"In several of his classes. I was an art major with a minor in psychology."

142

"Oh, I see."

"Elizabeth, I'm not going to take advantage of your friendship. I still want to see you professionally. Do you have some time on Monday or Tuesday?"

"You can come Monday afternoon, if you'd like. Just let me know when you feel like a professional visit." She knew it was against the rules to become friends with clients, but this case was an exception. If she had ever in her life met someone in need of a friend, it was Julie Waterford. And Elizabeth needed a friend as well.

"You've been very kind," Julie said in a soft voice. "And so has your husband. I really don't see why you two aren't together. I still miss Malcomb so very much."

Elizabeth sighed. "Maybe we can talk about that the next time I see you. Remember—not only are we neighbors, I'm only a phone call away."

"I know. If I start feeling too sad about Malcomb, I may give you a call. Weekends are the worst time for me. That's when we always puttered around the farm together."

Elizabeth tried to picture Michael *puttering* around Oak Shadows and failed. Still, he had taken pride in their small yard in back of the town house. He had kept the grass cut, even volunteered to prepare the soil for a small flower garden near the back porch, if she wanted one. But she hadn't had time then; she had been studying for finals.

"Well—" Elizabeth sat up straighter, trying to collect her thoughts—"see you on Monday, if not before."

After they said good-bye, Elizabeth felt much better about Julie. She was tempted to call Michael but resisted the urge. Instead, she opened a book she had purchased on antebellum homes. When the decorator came tomorrow she wanted to have a few ideas of her own to suggest.

Twenty

Saturday, October 5

A phone was ringing somewhere in the deep recesses of Michael's mind. He rolled over in bed with a groan, aware the ringing was not going to stop. He blinked sleepily at the bedside clock. It was 9 A.M. and his head had not hit the pillow until after two. He had spent more hours than he cared to, going from one popular lounge to another, looking for Johnni. To no avail.

He fumbled for the phone and breathed a weary hello.

"Hi, Michael," a deep sultry voice floated over the wire. "I have a message for Julie."

Michael bolted up, grabbing the pen and pad on his bedside table.

"Who is this?" he asked, copying the number displayed on the Caller ID: 770-553-l880.

"This is Johnni. We really should meet sometime. Tell Julie I've taken care of a big problem."

Michael was tugging off his pajamas, the phone cradled against his shoulder as he reached for his clothes.

"Johnni, why don't you meet me for lunch? We need to talk."

The line clicked. Michael pulled a sweater on over his head and stared at the phone for a minute. Then he redialed the number.

"Woodfield Nursing Home," a voice answered.

Michael frowned, puzzled. "Is this 553-l880?"

"Yes, it is. Who do you want?"

"Where have I called, please?"

"Woodfield Nursing Home," the voice repeated slowly, emphatically.

Michael glanced from the notepad to the Caller ID, pushing the review button. He had the right number. And the area code signified northwest Georgia.

"May I speak to Johnni, please?" he asked, totally puzzled.

"Who?"

Michael sighed, gravely fearing she had outsmarted him. "She's an attractive lady about thirty with short red hair."

"Hold on...." There was an interminable pause, during which he could hear voices in the background. He used that pause to finish dressing and was slipping his feet into Loafers when the voice came back on the line.

"One of the nurses saw a lady who looks like that. Want me to see if I can locate her? She's a visitor. I thought you were wanting an employee."

Michael tried to absorb this information as calmly as possible.

"Thank you very much for checking. No, you needn't bother trying to locate her. I'll talk to her later."

Michael rushed into the bathroom to freshen up, then hurried downstairs to the kitchen, reaching into the refrigerator to grab a carton of orange juice. Within minutes of the phone call, he was out the door, car keys in hand. Once he was behind the wheel of his car, he reached into the glove compartment for the state map he always carried. Woodfield was near Rome. He remembered Julie telling him that.

He wheeled out of the parking deck and headed for the interstate.

He was thankful that it was a Saturday morning, and many businesses were closed. Traffic had not yet clogged Interstate 75.

By using his radar scanner and being cautious, he was able to pull into Woodfield within an hour.

Glancing around, the little town was what he expected: one main street paralleling a post office, two groceries, a bank, and a clothing store, with a service station on each corner.

He slowed as he drove through the area, his eyes peeled for a certain redhead, but Woodfield was still asleep on this Saturday morning. As he approached the opposite end of town, he spotted a sign, Woodfield Nursing Home. The sign indicated a rambling, ranch-style structure with a wide front porch. He turned into the gravel drive leading up to the nursing home.

The parking lot, like the town, was not crowded. Several older-model cars were spaced about. Michael turned into the first space he came to and hopped out. Quickly, he scanned the license plates of the cars, although he couldn't imagine the flamboyant Johnni driving any vehicle he saw here. He turned and headed for the front door of the nursing home.

He opened the door and faced a long hallway. An antiseptic smell assaulted his nose. He started down the polished hall, glancing through open doors. From within the first room a young woman in a wheelchair by the window waved to Michael. He waved back.

At the second door, an old woman sat in a rocker, hugging a doll and staring blankly at a television screen featuring the morning cartoons.

At the third door, a frail, white-haired man lay in bed, staring at the ceiling.

Michael reached the nurses' station and hesitated, waiting for a round-faced nurse to look up from a file. When she didn't, he cleared his throat.

"Excuse me. I'm looking for Ms. Hankins."

She got up from the chair, and he noticed that her body was as round as her face. "You mean *Mr.* Hankins? He's in room 28. But he's being moved to the hospital. He suffered another stroke this morning and has gone into a coma."

Michael tried to retain his composure. "Mr. Hankins? Has his family been contacted?"

The nurse studied him curiously. His question obviously puzzled her. "He has no family."

Michael glanced up and down the hall, then looked back at the nurse. "I believe a Ms. Hankins came to see him this morning. She's a redhead about thirty and—"

"That woman wasn't family. She was from some agency in Atlanta."

Michael let that remark pass. "Do you know if she's left yet?"

She chewed a corner of her round lip, looking to the south of the hall. "I think so. You might check the social hall, though, just to be sure. Two doors down on the right."

"Thanks." Michael headed in that direction.

The social hall was a large rectangular room, with at least twenty elderly people huddled about—some in wheelchairs, some on sofas. A younger woman was playing a tune on the piano, something from the Glenn Miller era. Johnni was not in the social hall.

Michael continued on, scanning room numbers over the doors in search of 28. He located it at the far end of the south hall. The room was a semiprivate, with the two beds separated by a faded blue curtain. Around the bed nearest the door, there was a commotion.

A middle-aged woman wearing an RN tag on her white uniform hovered over the bed, while another nurse checked an oxygen tube.

When Michael looked at the man in the bed, he caught his breath. The man had once been tall, possibly heavy, judging from the deeply embedded wrinkles on his gray face. But now his body, like his face, appeared emaciated. His hair was red.

The RN spotted him. "Can I help you?"

"Excuse me," Michael replied, "but what happened to him?"

"May I ask who you are?" she asked, cocking an eyebrow.

"My name is Michael Calloway. I believe Mr. Hankins's daughter is here, or may have left. I'm looking for her."

The nurses exchanged puzzled glances, and the younger one shook her head. "He doesn't have any family," the younger nurse replied. "Or so we were told."

"Sir, I believe you have your people mixed up," the other nurse said brusquely. "Now if you'll excuse us." She turned back to the man, checking his pulse while she gazed at her watch.

Michael turned to the younger nurse, who seemed less occupied. She appeared to have done all she could to help. Noticing that Michael still lingered in the door, she took a step toward him, lowering her voice. "This man is indigent. He has no family."

Michael nodded slowly, deciding to try another approach.

"Maybe I'm confused. I have a friend, an attractive redhead, about thirty, who called me from this nursing home earlier."

The nurse frowned. "I didn't see her."

An ambulance was screaming into the back driveway. "They've come for him. Sir, you're blocking the door."

"I'm sorry," Michael mumbled, stepping back out of the way. He turned and retraced his steps down the hall, looking in other doors, although he knew there was no point. Johnni had been here to see her father, whether she admitted kinship or not. No doubt, her presence had brought on the stroke, but that was an opinion he would keep to himself, for now.

A plump little woman who looked to be in her seventies grabbed his arm.

"Herbert, I been waiting for you to come take me home."

"Sorry." He smiled down at her. "I'm not Herbert."

"Oh," she said, looking lost and confused.

Michael rushed out the front door, taking a deep gulp of the cool autumn air. He hesitated on the front porch, glancing around. The same people were still seated there, staring out at the parking lot, waiting for families to come visit. At the far end of the porch, however, a nicely dressed man in a dark suit was talking quietly with a thin little woman in a wheelchair.

Michael approached the man.

"Excuse me, sir, but did you know the Hankins man here at the nursing home?"

He took a step back from Michael, as though the words were some kind of warning. "I've heard of him. Back in the sixties, he almost cut my uncle's ear off in a fight. I've been gone from here for thirty years." He looked down at the older woman. "Mama, didn't you say the Hankins man was here? He'd be pretty old by now."

The older woman was nodding. "Yep, he's the crazy one at the end of the hall. Sally, my nurse, said that's who the ambulance came for. I heard her tell another nurse he'd bought the farm; don't know which farm they meant."

Michael would have thought the little woman's innocent remark humorous if the situation had not been grave.

"What about family?" Michael inquired.

The woman shook her head. "He has none."

"Do you know where he lived?" He looked back at the man.

The man scratched his head. "I think he still had a place out on the Coosa."

"Can you tell me how to get there?" Michael asked, feeling a spark of hope for the first time.

"Go back through town and hang a left at the fork of the road. Follow that road for…probably five miles. It'll turn to gravel, then dirt. The place I'm thinking of is the last thing you come to before you drop off in the river. I only know about it because during the summer when I used to visit Mama—" he nodded at the woman in the wheelchair—"I'd use Daddy's fishing boat and float down the river. I'd see Hankins out on his porch, drinking beer, looking mean." He shook his head. "I never liked the thought of him being in the same nursing home with Mama."

"Oh, Cecil! That man never got out of bed."

"Well, gotta go," Michael said. "You two have a nice day."

He hurried down the porch steps back to his Jeep. Johnni had been here; he knew it. Where was she now? He had a hunch she'd go back to the old place. He didn't know why; he just felt she would, out of curiosity, maybe.

Following the man's directions, he drove back through town and turned at the specified road. The woods thickened, and the potholes in the road increased with each mile. He couldn't imagine Julie Waterford living out in this desolate area. He passed a small, neat frame house where a woman was raking leaves. She looked up curiously as he passed, and he waved. Could this be the Bessie whom Julie had spoken of when she was frying chicken?

Another quarter mile and the road came to a dead end before a small gray shack, built on pilings, overlooking the river. There were no other vehicles around, but he could see fresh tire tracks in front of the house. Someone had been here recently.

He got out of the Jeep, wading through knee-high weeds to the shack. The windows were cracked, the front porch buckled.

He climbed up the rickety steps and knocked uselessly, then pushed open the creaking door.

He could smell a trace of cigarette smoke. He listened, peering around the small front room, which was layered with dust and cobwebs. Michael walked over to the fireplace. The old fireplace held a pile of soot—and a cigarette butt rimmed with vivid purple lipstick.

She *had* been here! Quickly, he completed his inspection of the shack, finding all the rooms in the same state of disrepair. Johnni had been here and gone. How close had he come to catching up with her?

He walked back out into the yard, glancing toward the river; then he hurried to his Jeep and jumped in behind the wheel. The woman in the yard—maybe she had seen Johnni's car pass and would remember it. *If I could get a description of the car, it would be a real break!* he thought, his pulse quickening.

He did a wide U-turn and headed back toward the last house he had passed. As he approached the picket fence, he slowed down and parked at the front gate.

The woman was still raking leaves. He jumped out of the car and walked through the gate and up the walkway.

"Good morning," he called.

"Mornin'." She was a heavyset woman dressed in a gray sweat suit. She had dark skin and short, curly hair.

"I'm looking for Bessie," he said, hoping this was the woman Julie had mentioned.

The woman grinned. "You found her. You sellin' insurance?"

He laughed. "No. I'm Julie Waterford's friend and—"

"*Julie?* How's my angel?"

"She's having a hard time, Bessie."

"That poor child always had a hard time," she said, shaking her head.

"I just came from their old place looking—"

"What on earth you doing there?" Her dark eyes widened in her round face. "Nothin' but bad luck ever came out of that place!"

"My name is Michael Calloway, and I'm a private investigator. Julie hired me to find Johnni."

"Julie hired you?" she asked, her mouth dropping open.

"That's right. Johnni has been calling her, bothering her, and I believe she was up at the old shack. I was wondering if you noticed a car pass while you were out in the yard. It would help if I knew what kind of car Johnni drives."

She turned her head, placing the rake against the side of the house. She shook her head, backing away from him. "I just came out in the yard about the time you passed. I can't talk to you now. I'm gettin' one of my headaches."

Michael stared curiously at her. Then, as she began to walk toward her porch, he called out, "Johnni's been here, hasn't she? You don't have to be afraid of her...."

"I'm not afraid. It's just this talk about the Hankins family. Gives me a headache every time."

"Wait!" Michael reached into his wallet for a business card. "Please let me leave my name and phone number with you. Call me if you see her again. You want to help Julie, don't you?"

Bessie hesitated, taking the card and staring at it. "Course I'd help Julie. Just let me think about this a little bit."

With that statement, she turned and went inside, closing the door.

Michael stood for a moment, staring at the closed door. He had read fear in her face—fear and worry.

Twenty-one

C arol Kingston stood in front of Elizabeth's house, her
hands on her hips, her short platinum hair thrown back
from her face as her eyes followed the graceful lines of
the house all the way up to the roof. Elizabeth stood beside her,
watching, waiting for her comments. She noted Carol's array of
gold jewelry, the red silk blouse and flaring navy slacks, navy
hose, and wedged heels. She was reputed to be an authority on
decorating homes like this one, but Elizabeth was dreading the
price tag attached. And she still had mixed emotions about
someone coming in and telling her how her homeplace should
be redone. She had some ideas of her own; she just wanted to
be sure she was not too far off base.

"How did this charming creation escape Sherman?" she
asked, turning blue eyes crinkled with fine lines back to
Elizabeth. "It's a question I always like to ask, since so many old
homes bear the ravages of fire or destruction."

"Well—" Elizabeth smiled—"according to family legend, my
great-great-grandmother managed to charm one of the Union
officers. She was also reputed to be a Confederate spy, so figure

that one out," she added, laughing.

"Sounds like a great story."

Elizabeth nodded. "It is, and someday I'd love to write about it. The locals like to claim that Jenny haunts the place now and then, checking things out."

Carol nodded. "But of course! Any respectable antebellum has its legendary ghost. It comes with the territory."

"I'd say it comes with the gossip. Sorry, but I believe dear Jenny is doing her walking on streets of gold."

Elizabeth could see she had lost Carol, who was already deep into her plans for Oak Shadows, no doubt.

"Ah, Elizabeth, I can just imagine this place with fresh paint, some bracing here and there. We could redo the landscaping." She whirled on Elizabeth. "What about the furnishings? I can imagine Chippendale highboys, Sheraton chairs, and—"

Elizabeth put a hand up. "There are still a few good pieces—console tables, washstands, armoires, a couple of silk window hangings. But I'm afraid the mirrors are smoked with age and—"

"What about gilt frames?"

"Oh, we do have those."

"Perfect. We can work with those."

"That's the point." Elizabeth looked directly at Carol. "I'd like to do as much as we can with what's here. You see, part of the charm of this place is my heritage here—the trunks in the attic, the scarred mahogany dining-room table, things that have been in the family for generations...."

"I understand completely. But with a house like this, there must have been valuable pieces." She bit her lip. "Sorry, I don't mean to pry."

"You aren't. My grandmother cherished all those pieces. Nonetheless, after she became old and ill with mounting debts, I'm afraid Mother needed money more than furniture. Many valuable pieces were sold, and since Grandmother was bedridden for the last two years of her life, she hardly knew what left the house."

"Oh, I see." Carol nodded, chewing the corner of her lip.

Elizabeth sighed. "I see beautiful antiques in stores, and it makes me ill. There were lovely things here that Mother chose to sell. But you see, my mother fell madly in love at eighteen and married rather quickly to a serviceman—my father—who was killed in Vietnam. She was devastated after that and, with me in tow, returned here for the security Oak Shadows offered. My grandfather had been dead for years, and Mother was an only child, like me," she added regretfully.

"You grew up here?"

Elizabeth nodded. "And I loved it. I suppose, in retrospect, I was always more like my grandmother than my mother. Mother had the soul of a dreamer. I suspect one reason Mother married a man who had chosen a career in the armed forces was so she could see the world. She adored traveling. The sad thing was, she never ventured far from here for many years. Then while I was away at private school, she met a wealthy man and married him. Now, at last, she's living her dreams and seeing the world. My last letter from her was postmarked *Dublin.*"

She finished her story, took a deep breath, and wrinkled her nose at Carol. "Now you know all the skeletons in our musty family closet."

Carol laughed at the expression. "I'm glad you explained. And I think it's admirable of you to want to come back here and restore this lovely place." A tiny frown marred her perfect brow. "I can see there will be a lot of work involved."

Elizabeth nodded. "More on the outside than within. The rooms are pretty much intact. The structure is sound, even though many of the papered walls have been painted. I'll warn you in advance that you won't like the paint. I wish Mother had stayed with the antebellum look rather than going for comfort, although she chose the practical approach, I suppose. The consequence is that we now have a sixties color scheme wrapped in columns and verandahs. It's pretty funny when you think about it!"

They both laughed as Carol turned back to her station wagon. "I brought along some books for you to see. And some swatches of fabric, paint samples, all those fun things. You'll have plenty to mull over."

Elizabeth's brow arched at the armload of goodies Carol was pulling out of the backseat.

"Here, let me help. These may take years to mull over," Elizabeth said, already bewildered by so many choices. "And in the end, you'll probably be the one to make the decisions, Carol. As I told you over the phone, I'm almost as blind as my mother was to decorating. I do know what feels right—I just don't know how to accomplish it."

"I understand." Carol nodded, gripping the books with ruby acrylic nails and dangling gold bracelets. Elizabeth could see that Carol was very prosperous in her work. It occurred to her that she should have an understanding about expenses.

"My grandmother set up a trust fund for me years ago, which became available at her death. I want to use the money to restore Oak Shadows. However, I must warn you in advance that I have a limit on expenses."

"Want to give me an idea of the limit?" Carol asked, coming right to the point.

Elizabeth sighed. "I'm putting some back for Katie, but I can spend around fifty thousand. No more."

Carol frowned, then nodded. "We can work with that."

Work with that? Elizabeth still was not reassured, but at least Carol knew how much could be allotted for this job. *Might as well get on with it*, she decided. "I have a pot of tea steeping in the kitchen. Let's head back there, and maybe you can tell me what you've done in some other homes, for starters."

"Good idea." Carol's platinum head bobbed. "What a great fanlight over the door," she said, staring in appreciation.

As they lugged the books inside, Elizabeth watched, half amused, as Carol's expression of interest alternated between approval and horror, approval and horror.

Elizabeth laughed. "I warned you this was not going to be an easy job."

"I believe you may be right," Carol said, staring wide-eyed at the odd mixture of old and new thrown together. Elizabeth was glad that her mother now chose to have someone else do the decorating in her homes.

Twenty-two

This was turning into a long Saturday for Michael. He had driven from Woodfield back to the Waterford farm to speak with Julie. In his haste to catch up with Johnni, he had run out without the magnetic phone directory he always kept over his visor. When he tried Elizabeth's house, hoping to get Julie's number, all he got was the answering machine.

"Hi, it's me," he spoke to the machine. "I'm on my way to Julie Waterford's house. Will stop by your place coming or going." He paused, glancing at his watch. "It's now one o'clock," he said, "and I expect to be there around two. Talk to you later."

This was not his weekend to pick up Katie, yet he wanted to see her. And he wanted to see Elizabeth.

With the window down, he breathed deeply of the fresh autumn air, trying to clear away the memory of mold and must from the shack, and the smell of medicine and illness at the nursing home.

~~~~~~

Since he had to pass the Waterford farm before getting to Elizabeth's house, he turned in, hoping to catch Julie at home. He knew she rarely left. He pulled up the driveway and parked the Jeep, looking around. The front door opened, and Julie stood there.

"Hi," he called as he got out of the car. "Sorry to drop by unannounced, but I left home in a hurry. Got a minute?"

"Sure," she said, looking puzzled. She sat down in a porch chair and motioned him to another one.

She looked better to him than before. She wore a soft pink slacks outfit that complimented her figure, although he thought she was too thin. The only flaw in her appearance was the fact that her hair was slightly mussed, and her eyes were a bit red. Had she lost sleep, or had she been crying?

"Have you heard from Johnni?" he asked.

She shook her head. "No, but I unplugged the phone. I've been asleep," she said, rubbing her eyes.

"Well, I have definitely heard from her," he said, watching her expression.

Her brown eyebrows arched. "You have? When did she call? What did she say? And how did she find you?"

"Good question."

"Wait a minute!" She jumped from the chair. "Let me check on something."

She hurried through the front door. What had she thought of? Within seconds, she was back on the porch. "I put your business card under a magnet on my refrigerator, with a dozen others. I hadn't noticed, but it's gone. She must have taken it when she came here and tore the place apart."

Michael said nothing. He didn't want her to know what he was thinking. His eyes roamed slowly around the property.

Johnni must be somewhere near, keeping an eye on Julie. She knew who he was and how to find him. And if she knew that, she knew about Elizabeth and Katie. He didn't like the idea.

"Julie, your sister called me from a nursing home in Woodfield. I went there.... She had already left...but I saw your father," he added gently.

Julie stared at him. "My father is living in Key West. I told you that earlier. He and Mother—"

"No, I meant your biological father. I checked my Caller ID when she phoned me. The call came from Woodfield Nursing Home, so I jumped in the car and took off up there. A woman with red hair had been there, but I missed her. But Mr. Hankins..." His voice trailed off as he watched Julie's face turn pale.

"Wait." She pressed a hand to her forehead, closing her eyes. "You're confusing me. You're saying she knew where Bull was...that she went there to see him."

"Yes. He suffered a stroke this morning. He was already in critical condition, from what I gathered. Now, he may not—"

She put a hand up. "I don't want to hear about him. I don't care where he is. He was a very cruel man, Michael. I can't think of him without getting sick." She swallowed, tears welling in her eyes. "I left that behind years ago. Please don't rehash that period of my life...or him. I just can't do it." She shook her head as a tear slipped down her cheek.

"I'm sorry, Julie. I didn't mean to upset you. I just wanted you to know what was going on. And I think you should know that Johnni went to the...place you once lived. I found another vivid purple cigarette butt in the fireplace, and there was still smoke in the air."

Her wet brown eyes lifted to him, and when he saw her torment, he was tempted to drop the subject. Still, she had to know about Johnni; after all, this was why she had hired him.

163

"I saw Bessie," he said, more gently.

"Bessie." The word was spoken with such tenderness that Michael knew at least he had found a better subject.

"She asked me how you were doing."

"Bessie was my best friend there. I'd like to see her."

Michael nodded. "She certainly seems fond of you." He decided not to mention the fear he had read in her face, or the fact that he suspected Johnni had been to see her, possibly threatened her. Knowing that would not help Julie feel better.

"Well, I just wanted to update you," he said, coming to his feet.

"Are you going to see Elizabeth now?"

He nodded, shoving his hands in his pockets. "As a matter of fact, I am. I'll be there for a while before heading back into Atlanta. Are you sure you're okay? Want to come with me to visit Elizabeth?"

She shook her head. "No, I don't want to leave home. Thank you."

The afternoon breeze rippled through the big oaks, and Michael looked from the trees to the beautiful lawns. "This is really a pretty place," he said, surveying the grounds. It was a shame she couldn't be happy here, but heartache seemed to stalk her wherever she went.

"Oak Shadows will be just as pretty when Elizabeth finishes her work on it. You should move up here."

He glanced down at her, but she had tucked her head, and a slight flush was creeping over her cheeks.

"I'm sorry. I don't mean to be prying into your and Elizabeth's life," she said.

He heaved a sigh. "Don't worry about it, Julie. You aren't prying. Well, see you later. And remember, we'll find her."

She nodded, watching him carefully as he walked back to his Jeep.

"Michael," she called to him, walking forward to lean against one of the columns that rose gracefully to the roof. "Our birthday is Friday."

He nodded. "I know."

They stared at one another for a moment. He wondered what she was thinking; he hoped her thoughts were not as troubled as his. There was a sense of urgency to every case he took, but this one had really started to bother him. He didn't like being taunted, and Johnni was definitely doing that—not just to Julie, but now to him as well. It was a cat-and-mouse game, and he had a feeling she was enjoying herself thoroughly.

He got in the Jeep without further comment. He didn't want to upset Julie more. She had seemed better, until he mentioned locating her biological father. He didn't even want to think about two little girls living in that shack, reeking with poverty, and a man who Julie acknowledged had been a bully. What had he done to them? What horrible secrets lay buried within Julie's delicate state of mind?

Twenty-three

With thoughts of Julie still hovering in his head, he drove faster, needing to see Katie more than ever. What if they were still gone? What if—

Slowing up, he glanced right to left, admiring the red and gold touches on the big trees, trying to calm himself before he arrived at their door like a wild man. As he turned in and drove toward the house, his eyes widened. A black Cadillac was parked in the driveway.

Recalling how Johnni had stayed one step ahead of him brought a pang of concern. He came to a quick stop, turned off the engine, and hopped out.

As he climbed the porch steps, a wonderful aroma drifted through a half-open window in the room that was Elizabeth's office. Since cooking was not Elizabeth's strong point, he began to wonder if her mother and stepfather were back from Europe. He hesitated, then felt ridiculous. He would not allow his mother-in-law to intimidate him, as he had in the past.

Squaring his shoulders, he rang the doorbell and waited. He could hear footsteps along the hallway, and then the door opened and he was facing a woman he had never seen. She was a tall, middle-aged woman with brown hair and eyes. She wore tan slacks and a white sweater covered with a bright red apron.

"Hello," she said pleasantly.

"Hello, I'm Michael Calloway. I just stopped by to see Elizabeth and Katie."

"Oh, I'm so sorry you've missed them, Mr. Calloway. I'm Grace Binkley," she said as pushed the door open, extending her hand. "Elizabeth has been such a dear to help me out at the hospital, so I offered to cook dinner tonight. Elizabeth and Katie have gone into Atlanta with the decorator to select some fabric. Frankly—" she grinned—"I believe Elizabeth may have bribed Katie with a stop-off at the mall if she would tag along with them."

"I see," he replied, though he didn't.

"Would you like to come in and wait?"

The decorator.

When he hesitated, she continued smoothly, "You're welcome to join us for dinner. There's plenty of food, and the decorator is staying."

He shook his head quickly. "No, thank you anyway." He hesitated, thinking of Katie again. "I'd like to leave some money for Katie though."

"How nice." She beamed at him. "You caught what I said about the mall, didn't you?"

He smiled. She was a very nice lady, one he would enjoy getting to know, but he was still bothered about the decorator business.

"I know how Katie likes to shop," he said, removing his wallet.

"If you want to leave her some money, feel free to go on up to her room. I'll tell her it's on the dresser."

"Okay." He smiled as he entered the hall.

"I need to check something in the oven," she called over her shoulder.

He turned and glanced up at the staircase, recalling the first time he had come here with Elizabeth during their courtship. They were both living in Atlanta when a mutual friend introduced them at a party. Elizabeth was attending Agnes Scott, and he was working on the police force.

With little in common except their Christian beliefs and a longing for home and family, they fell in love that first week, after long, leisurely talks. Their courtship continued throughout the summer.

She brought him up here to meet her grandmother. He thought she was a sweet lady, far more personable than her daughter, Elizabeth's mother, who hadn't bothered to conceal her disapproval of his profession.

"What line of work are you in?" Elizabeth's mother had asked abruptly.

"I'm opening my own detective agency," he had answered politely.

"A detective agency? *Oh...*"

He and Elizabeth returned to Oak Shadows on other occasions, even spent the night here in one of the bedrooms upstairs. He remembered thinking it was the biggest house he had ever seen. He was uncomfortable in it then, just as he was now.

He climbed the stairs slowly, his head tilted upward, taking in the massive chandelier. He doubted that his dad had ever seen anything like it in his life. He couldn't care less either.

On the second level, he peered into the first room, obviously Elizabeth's room, because he could see her jeans and shirt on a chair. And there were other touches, distinctly Elizabeth.

The high-ceilinged room was spacious enough to contain a lot of furniture. This must have been the master bedroom. A four-poster and a night table were placed beside the window. He remembered that Elizabeth liked rolling over and looking out a window first thing in the morning. He forced his eyes toward the other furnishings. A French Provincial chair looked oddly out of place, but the rich patina of the armoire compensated for everything else, even the fading wallpaper that was peeling slightly at the corners.

Since he was free to enter the room unobserved, he wandered toward the bed, staring first at the needlepoint pillow Elizabeth had done last year. Beside the bed the night table held a few eloquent ornaments, but he was more interested in the photograph than anything else in the room.

The frame held an eight-by-ten snapshot of Michael, Elizabeth, and Katie at the beach.

Pain filled his heart. If Elizabeth no longer cared for him, why did she keep his picture beside her bed? Staring at the picture, he noted the way the three of them cuddled together on a beach blanket. Would they ever be together that way again?

Suddenly, ten years' worth of memories rushed through his mind as tears filled his eyes. She was still his wife. Neither had made any move toward a divorce because each believed in keeping the promises of marriage. *So what's going to happen?* he wondered.

He turned and walked out of the bedroom and down the hall to the next room, obviously Katie's room. He sniffed and smiled to himself at the look and smell of Katie. Her white French Provincial bedroom set had been left at the town house. Elizabeth had chosen to use the furnishings that were already here.

A bitter grin tugged at his lips. The thought behind the action was some weird loyalty to Michael on Elizabeth's part. On his salary, he couldn't purchase any more furniture; what they owned at the town house was relatively inexpensive, compared to the antiques that filled this place.

The room Katie used was the one that once belonged to Elizabeth. There were no antiques here, just lots of long windows with nice views. Twin beds held matching pink ruffled bedspreads, and pink Priscilla curtains outlined the windows. The wallpaper was newer, a pink-and-blue plaid.

Michael turned to her dresser, where a variety of ribbons cluttered the surface. He placed some money between a silver brush and comb and reluctantly turned away, needing to escape the pain that had taken root in Elizabeth's room and was now spreading rapidly.

He headed back downstairs, not wanting to see any more of the house where Elizabeth and Katie now lived. They seemed to be managing okay on their own. He knew he could be useful to them here, helping with the repairs, just keeping them company, grilling steaks while the "girls" tossed a salad, or donning the chef's apron Elizabeth had given him and preparing the special barbecue chicken they both loved. But they were living without him now. And, furthermore, they were doing okay.

Downstairs, Grace Binkley entered the hall from the kitchen. "Sure you won't stay to eat?" she asked again.

He shook his head. "No, thank you very much. It was nice meeting you." He flashed her a smile and hurried out the front door. Once he was inside his Jeep, all the frustration that had been festering concentrated itself in his foot as he pressed the accelerator and sped down the drive, swerving back on the two-lane. A decorator had replaced him. A decorator and old family money.

When Michael returned home there was a message on his machine from Tommy.

"Hi, Michael. I located a salesgirl in one of the cosmetic

171

departments in Macy's at Lennox Mall. She sells this weird lipstick and remembers the redhead. She can't remember when
she came in—said it was weeks ago. But she definitely remembers her. Paid cash, so there's no address."

Michael felt his hopes dashed when he heard the last bit of
information. Thwarted again!

"I left my name and phone number. If Johnni comes back,
the salesgirl promised to call me."

Michael shook his head. Every time they got close, they lost
her. Still, it was only a matter of time until they caught up. He
glanced at the calendar and raked nervously through his hair.
Time was running out. Julie and Johnni's birthday was Friday.

Twenty-four

Elizabeth lay in her bed, feeling a strange mood slip over her. She and Katie had spent the day in Atlanta with the decorator, selecting fabric for upholstery, paper for the walls, some oriental rugs to overlay the hardwood floors. She was giddy with excitement when she returned home.

Her excitement turned to appreciation when they sat down to sample Grace Binkley's marvelous roast and potatoes. But then her spirits began a downward spiral. Grace Binkley informed her that Michael had stopped by to leave some money for Katie. He had not bothered to wait for them, even though Grace assured her she had insisted he stay for dinner.

Elizabeth was unable to analyze just why that bothered her, but it did. She should have realized he would be too stubborn to stay a minute longer than necessary. But why had he come?

Julie Waterford!

She grabbed the phone on her table and quickly dialed the number. A sleepy-sounding Julie answered after several rings.

"Julie, I've awakened you. I'm sorry. This is Elizabeth."

"Hi, Elizabeth."

"Did Michael stop by your place today?"

"Yes, he did. He said Johnni had called him, and he was trying to track her down."

"Johnni called him?" Elizabeth gasped.

"His business card is missing from my refrigerator."

"So what did Johnni say to him?"

There was a momentary pause. "He said the number on his Caller ID showed a nursing home up in Woodfield."

"Woodfield? You mean Johnni called from Woodfield?"

"Apparently. When he called the number back…" Her voice trailed off, and there was a pause. "Elizabeth, I'm about to get into some things that we need to talk about during my appointment Monday. To give you the bottom line, she was already gone when he got there. Basically, that's what he came to tell me."

Elizabeth frowned, not liking the answer. He could have called to tell her that. Why had he made the trip to Waterford Farm, and then here?

"I'll see you on Monday, Julie," Elizabeth said softly. "Sorry I woke you."

After she replaced the phone, she crossed her arms and stared across the bed to the chest of drawers. What had he found at Woodfield? Why couldn't Julie talk about it now?

Automatically, her hand reached for the phone again, then hesitated. Grace had said he only stopped by to leave some money for Katie, and Katie's squeal of delight had confirmed that. As usual, it was still business. Why did she hope he might have come to see her?

And what were they going to do about their marriage?

She slumped into the pillow, feeling sick at heart. Professionally, she needed to know what he had discovered at Woodfield so she'd be prepared for her session with Julie on Monday. But her heart ached with hurt, and as she looked at the empty space in the bed that Michael had shared, tears filled her eyes and rolled down her cheeks.

She so wanted to keep her marriage vows, but the separation between them seemed to be widening every day.

CHAPTER

Twenty-five

Sunday, October 6

Michael had been tempted to lounge in bed with the newspaper and remote control, traveling no further than the kitchen for more coffee and juice. He had, however, dragged himself out in time to shower and dress for the eleven o'clock church service. Something deep in his heart rebelled, for God did not seem to be answering his prayers. He prayed each night that he and Elizabeth could solve their problems, that with Katie they could be a family again.

"Be patient," his mother had told him when she called to discuss the problem one evening this week.

"Mom, you know patience isn't one of my characteristics."

"That's why you're getting a lesson in it," she replied. Then her voice softened, and she assured him that she loved him and that she was claiming in faith a reunion for his little family. "Just give God time," she said.

He remembered Elizabeth reading an autobiography about a miracle coming to pass after giving God time to work things out. *Maybe that's the way it will happen for us*, he thought hopefully as he adjusted his tie and gave himself a once-over in the mirror. But in his heart, he knew they must make some effort on their own. What was the old saying? God helps those who help themselves. Attending the Promise Keepers meeting had been a start. And the book he was reading concerned rebuilding a broken marriage. One of the points the book made was to get counseling from a pastor or reliable counselor before it was too late.

Maybe he would mention this to Elizabeth.

As he grabbed his Bible and hurried off for church, he thought of Jay and Promise Keepers. Perhaps there were other books. He could even pass them on to Elizabeth if she was receptive. Instead of spending the afternoon at the office or playing couch potato with the television set, he might read another book. Maybe he would find something to help his situation.

Elizabeth and Katie had gone to church, stopped off at a quaint little restaurant for lunch, and returned home shortly before two. Hoping for a long, leisurely nap, Elizabeth had changed into comfortable clothes and was eyeing her bed longingly when the telephone rang.

"Elizabeth," Julie's voice came in a rush. "She's calling me again. Is it possible for you to see me this afternoon rather than tomorrow?"

"You mean now?" Elizabeth asked, staring regretfully at the bed.

"Yes. Now, if it's possible."

Elizabeth forced a polite tone to her voice. "Sure." She never worked on Sunday, but in this situation, she was afraid to say no. When Johnni called, it meant trouble. "Come on over now, if you want."

Julie ran out the front door, never bothering to check the alarm system or the lock, jumped into her Mercedes, and drove toward Elizabeth's house. Her palms were moist against the steering wheel, and her breath was coming in gasps. That same terror was seizing her again, that sense of anxiety and panic.

She could no longer talk to Malcomb about her problems. That only left Elizabeth Calloway. She was in trouble and she knew it.

She swerved into the driveway and slammed the brakes on, jerking the big car to a halt. Turning the key in the ignition, she glanced down at her clothes, aware for the first time how tousled she looked. *Does Elizabeth have company on Sundays?* she wondered, glancing around the driveway. There were no cars other than Elizabeth's Honda.

She peered into the mirror over the visor, smoothing her short brown hair with trembling hands. Her face was as pale as ever, and she hadn't bothered with mascara or lip gloss. She rarely did, these days.

She was wearing jeans and a sweatshirt, something her adoptive mother would have considered inappropriate for a Sunday visit, but she had not thought about changing. All she could think about was getting to Elizabeth.

Elizabeth opened the door to a nervous-looking Julie and was glad she had agreed to see her.

"Hi, come on in." She tried to sound composed and casual.

They walked into the office, and Elizabeth closed the door behind them, having warned Katie not to interrupt. The phones were already switched to the answering machine, so they would not be disturbed.

Julie made a dash for the Queen Anne chair as Elizabeth took a seat behind her desk, her hands folded on the blotter.

"You look very concerned, Julie. What's going on?"

Julie swallowed and took a few seconds to speak. She was taking deep breaths, obviously trying to calm herself. "Yesterday, when Michael went to Woodfield to the nursing home, Johnni had been there. He told me—" she hesitated, grabbed another breath, and plunged on—"that Bull was dying. Apparently, he suffered a stroke after Johnni's visit. Out of curiosity, I called up there this morning. He…died last night."

Elizabeth stared at Julie, taking in the information she had heard. "I'm sorry," she replied.

"Then this morning, while I was still asleep, I heard something."

"Heard something?"

"I was still half asleep when I heard Johnni. She said, 'Have you told them how Horn-Rims died?'"

Julie dropped her head, taking deep breaths.

"Wait a minute, Julie, I'm lost. You heard Johnni where? In the house?"

"On the phone. I was so sound asleep I must have answered the phone without realizing it. I had the phone in my hand, but then the line had clicked."

"Horn-Rims?" Elizabeth echoed. "What on earth did she mean by that?"

"Malcomb wore glasses with dark rims. You know, the kind you'd jokingly refer to as horn-rims. One other time when she was taunting me, she referred to him as Horn-Rims."

Something was ticking in the back of Elizabeth's mind, a clue she could not yet name. She got out of the chair, crossed her arms, and looked down at Julie.

"He wasn't wearing glasses in the portrait."

"No, he only wore them for reading."

Elizabeth nodded, chewing her lip. "Had Johnni ever met Dr. Waterford?"

"Not to my knowledge. Not unless she stalked him like she's stalking me."

Elizabeth shoved her hands in the pockets of her baggy jeans, her mind clicking. "You say your husband only wore glasses for reading. He would have worn them at work, looking over charts, that sort of thing."

"Yes, that's right." Julie looked up at her, bewildered.

Elizabeth turned to Julie. "Is it possible Johnni had been a patient of his?"

Julie leaned back in the chair, her brown eyes widening. "He would have told me. If he knew she was my sister."

"It's possible she didn't tell him that. It's also possible that she went to see him professionally, just out of curiosity, to see the type of man you had married." She shook her head. "I don't think we should rule anything out, Julie."

Julie was shaking her head. "But I didn't hear from her until after Malcomb died."

Suddenly, both women were silent. A terrible thought crossed Elizabeth's mind. She watched Julie's face pale even more. Would the same thought occur to Julie? she wondered.

"Tell me what you're thinking, Julie."

Julie shook her head, staring into space.

"All right, then may I tell you what crossed my mind? You mentioned there was another car involved in the accident that killed Malcomb. The other car was never located." There was a deep, meaningful pause. Julie had covered her eyes with her hand. "Is it possible Johnni could have been driving the other car?" Elizabeth asked slowly.

"No," Julie replied, her voice muffled behind her hand. "No, it isn't possible. She's not a murderer."

She removed her hand and looked at Elizabeth, her eyes

181

shimmering with unshed tears. "She might be mean, and she was always a prankster, but—"

"A prankster? Is that what you call the mess she made at your house? Merely a prank?" Elizabeth was getting frustrated. Why couldn't Julie see the truth? Her twin was a very dangerous woman, with her capabilities far exceeding that of a mere prank.

Julie shook her head. "I wasn't thinking of that. I was thinking back to our childhood. The last prank she pulled...the one that..."

She stopped talking, placing the back of her hand to her mouth.

Elizabeth circled her desk and sat down. Whatever was going through Julie's mind now was meaningful; she was certain of that. *The last prank...the one...*She couldn't let Julie stop now; she had to stay after her, find out what she was thinking. She was certain something important had not been said.

"Talk to me. What did she do?"

Julie took a deep, quivering breath. When she spoke, her voice was little more than a whisper. "One day Johnni strung baling wire across the porch steps. The porch was built on stilts because we lived near the river. When Bull came out, he tripped on the wire and fell down the steps."

"Was he hurt?"

"Just angry. He found the wire. I guess Johnni thought he wouldn't figure it out...."

"And then?"

"I'd never seen him so angry. He started looking for her. I ran out of the house to the woods, hiding from him. I knew where she was hiding, but I didn't want him to find her." Her hands were trembling and she clenched them tightly. "He did find her, though. I could hear from the woods." She stared into space, tears slipping down her cheeks. "I'll never forget the sound of her screams."

Elizabeth sank deeper into her chair, feeling sick at heart herself. How had either girl survived?

"Was that when the social worker was called in?" she asked gently.

"About that time." Julie seemed preoccupied, almost resigned to her fate.

"Julie, what is it? You aren't giving up, are you?"

"We just don't seem to be getting anywhere. I'm not referring to you and me; it's the investigation. Don't misunderstand. I'm not saying your husband isn't a good investigator. It's just that stopping Johnni isn't going to be easy. I told you that in the beginning."

Elizabeth nodded thoughtfully. "I know you did. But don't give up on Michael just yet. He usually comes through. Sometimes the breaks don't work until the last minute, but he's the best, and that's not just my opinion."

Julie looked across at her, not smiling, but rather patiently observing. "Is it possible you're prejudiced?"

Elizabeth shrugged. "It's possible. But one of the reasons we're separated is his devotion to his work and his loyalty to his clients. He told me you now have priority. I think you should feel encouraged."

Julie thought about that. "I suppose so."

Elizabeth picked up a pen, rolling it between her palms. "Let's give him credit for what he's doing right. After all, he tracked Johnni to Woodfield. In fact, he was only a few steps behind her."

Julie shrugged. "So he said."

Elizabeth frowned. "Don't you believe him?"

"Yes, I believe him. Otherwise, how would he know of…the man's condition?"

Elizabeth studied Julie carefully. She wore no makeup; her hair was slicked back from her pale face. Even her lips looked bloodless. She was not a healthy woman at this point. Defeat shadowed her eyes, the expression on her face, the rumpled clothing. She would now be a very easy target for her aggressive sister. And that really worried Elizabeth.

Furthermore, she no longer called her biological father Bull. She referred to him as "he" or "the man." Did that mean the pain was too great for her even to speak his nickname? Elizabeth had to get to the bottom of this, but she wasn't sure she could do that with Julie.

Elizabeth squeezed the pen in her palm, trying to think what to say.

"Julie, may I ask you a question?"

Julie hesitated. "What is it?"

"How did you feel about Michael going up to the nursing home in Woodfield?"

Julie frowned. "I'm not sure."

"But what if he had caught up with Johnni?"

"He didn't. Perhaps that's the problem I'm having. He always seems to get so close; then he loses her."

"He won't lose her," Elizabeth said emphatically. "She's going to make a mistake. She already has." She decided not to elaborate on that.

Julie's doubtful expression prompted Elizabeth to try a change of subject. "Did you think about coming with me to the little Bible study I mentioned? It meets on Wednesday evenings."

"No, I don't think I want to do that." Her eyes roamed around the room as if she wanted to avoid the subject completely.

She seemed less shy, more impatient today. The strain of the past months was obviously beginning to show.

Julie looked back at Elizabeth and her eyes softened. "Maybe later, when some of my personal problems are behind me, I can go to your Bible study. I'd actually like to try and understand your faith, or whatever it is that motivates you to be the kind of person you are."

"Okay, come when you feel up to it. But let me assure you of one thing: I find my strength through studying the Bible, praying, and being together with other Christians. I know that could be a help to you."

Julie looked across at Elizabeth, showing a flash of emotion for the first time. "I guess that goes back to how a person is raised. My mother and father, the Harrises, seemed to have a belief in a greater being, but they never actually talked to me about it, other than in generalities. And I don't recall their ever going to church." She hesitated, dropping her eyes to her hands. "*He* didn't believe in God, and the women in his life who came and went didn't seem to believe in anything except their sexuality. There was one person, however, someone I always loved and respected, who used to speak of her God."

"Who was that person, may I ask?"

Julie's pale lips tilted in a half smile. "It was Bessie, our closest neighbor. She exemplified all that was good and right; sometimes she was the only real friend I had. Bessie was a believer," she finished quietly.

"What about Malcomb?" Elizabeth asked, curious for the first time.

Julie took a deep breath. "Malcomb was an agnostic. This, obviously, didn't strengthen my faith. But I respected Malcomb so very much. Elizabeth, let me ask your opinion on something." She looked at Elizabeth curiously. "Malcomb had a theory that everyone has a dark side, that when we refuse to acknowledge our dark side we become sick."

Elizabeth chewed her lip. "That's interesting. What's your dark side?"

"Fear. It keeps me locked within the walls of my house."

"And what do you think about Johnni?"

"She's very dark."

Elizabeth nodded. "Too bad she never saw your husband professionally."

"She wouldn't have. She would have resented Malcomb because I married him. She would imagine that he was being condescending to her. But I believe he could have helped her. He helped me."

"How?"

"He gave me confidence." She sighed. "But I'm losing that confidence." She sank lower in the chair. "Just as I seem to be losing everything else."

"Julie, don't say that. You're going through a rough time, but you're going to make it. I'm going to help you."

"Thanks," Julie responded. But her eyes lacked conviction. She rose from the chair, swaying slightly.

Elizabeth came around the desk, bracing Julie's shoulders with her hands. "It's okay. You've told me some important things today. And by telling me, you've released some dark memories from your mind for a while. Perhaps this will even help with your nightmares."

All the life seemed to have been drained from Julie. Standing beside her now, Elizabeth thought she seemed to have lost more weight in the past week. She judged her to be no more than ninety-eight pounds.

"Let me fix us some tea. Come out to the kitchen."

Julie shook her head tiredly. "I just want to go home, Elizabeth. I need to go to bed."

"All right. I'll call and check on you later." She put an arm around her shoulder and walked her to the door.

Julie didn't bother saying good-bye as she dragged herself across the porch and down the front steps. Elizabeth watched her get into the Mercedes and start the engine. She looked so small and frail, so helpless. Such an easy target for Johnni.

As she turned back to her office, her thoughts began to race. What kind of monster had Johnni become? Was it possible that she was, in fact, responsible for the accident that killed Malcomb Waterford?

Katie dressed for church on Sunday evening, her Bible in her hand, her hair swept back in a mini-ponytail. She liked the Bible study they had on Sunday evenings, and she hurried down the steps to find her mother sitting in the office and staring into space.

"Mom, have you forgotten about church?"

Elizabeth looked at her blankly for a minute, then jumped to her feet. "I'll be ready in ten minutes. And Katie..." She hesitated, thinking. "Let's stay for that ice-cream social afterwards. You and I need to spend more time together, have some fun."

Katie grinned. "Sure, Mom. But hurry—I don't want to be late. Everyone stares when you're late."

Twenty-six

Michael had stopped by Tommy and Tina's place for coffee and a chat about the mysterious Johnni. The lab's report had been discouraging. The fingerprints were smudged, thanks to Julie's help in scooping them up. Their only hope now was that Johnni had a record—or that Tommy could turn her up from the sketch.

Michael had even made a late afternoon sweep of the nearest mall after reading for a couple of hours. He had gotten nowhere.

When he arrived back at his dark town house that night, a deep emptiness seemed to penetrate his heart. He felt they were making some progress with finding Johnni, but everything was moving too slowly. After all, they only had five days to go.

He walked into the kitchen, needing coffee. When he looked around, the room looked as though no one lived there. Certainly, he never ate at home. The room looked sterile, impersonal, except for a well-used coffeemaker and the chipped mug Katie had given him last Father's Day. He measured coffee, switched on the coffeemaker, and reached for the mug.

He stared at the printing on the mug. WORLD'S GREATEST DAD.

"Yeah, right," he mumbled.

The phone rang, prompting him out of his thoughts, and he made a dive for it.

"Hi, Dad."

The sound of his daughter's voice softened his heart. "Hi, sweetheart. What's up?"

"I'm being baptized next Sunday night. Can you come up?"

"You're being baptized?" he repeated, delighted by the news. "Sure, I can come. What time is the baptism?"

She hesitated. "I'm not sure. Here, you better talk to Mom."

He held the phone back from his ear as she shouted for her mother. He could hear the tap of Elizabeth's steps across the hardwood floor, and the echo of mumbled voices in the background.

"Hi," she said.

"Hi. Katie tells me she's being baptized next Sunday evening. I want to be there."

"That's very sweet, Michael," Elizabeth said. "The service is at seven, and the baptism follows. Would you like to come for a salad around six?"

"Sure. Let's just hope and pray we'll have found Johnni by then," Michael said. "But I don't want to mention anything unpleasant in the same breath with Katie's good news. I'm glad she's being baptized." He hesitated, then added, "Thanks for calling."

Feeling better after the phone call, Michael went over and slouched down in his recliner, propping his feet up, thinking about how fast the years had gone since Katie had been born.

Just then the telephone rang, and he glanced at the Caller ID. It showed the number for the "Sun Dial Lounge." He grabbed it.

He glanced at his watch. Seven-thirty.

"Mr. Calloway, this is Marty, the hostess at the Sun Dial. Your lady's here. Came in alone about five minutes ago."

Michael bolted out of his chair. "I'm on my way. Don't let her out of your sight."

Michael jumped into his Jeep and screeched out of the parking deck. Cutting around cars, switching lanes, driving as fast as he dared, he reached the entrance to the Peachtree Hotel parking deck in record time.

Braking at the valet station, he hopped out and tossed his keys to a valet.

"Park it close," he called. "I may leave in a hurry."

The valet was obviously amused. "Busy night, sir?"

"I hope so."

Michael was breathless as he hurried toward the lounge, parting his hair with his fingers, glancing down and realizing belatedly that he was dressed too casually for this type of place. He hadn't time to worry about his wardrobe, however.

As he entered the dim lounge, he could see it was crowded this evening with singles and couples chatting and sipping drinks.

Marty walked up to him. "Around the corner, first table to the left. A man just joined her."

Michael shoved several bills in Marty's palm, then began

looking around, attempting to appear casual.

The lounge had a merry-go-round effect as Michael moved in the opposite direction of the revolving bar. Candlelight reflected against the glass walls, with a backdrop of starry sky.

He turned a corner and spotted a table for two by the window. A distinguished-looking businessman was looking across to a redhead, who was seated with her back to Michael.

Michael walked on past the table, looking straight ahead until he was several feet away. Then he glanced casually over his shoulder.

Wisps of red hair tickled her cheek, and bangs tumbled low on her forehead. She wore a low-cut black dress, and her mouth was a vivid purple. He tried to make a quick study of her, but suddenly her emerald eyes lifted and looked directly at him. A shock ran through him. It *was* her—and she spotted him!

Quickly, he turned his back to her and began to walk on, trying to collect his thoughts. What was the best way to approach her? What should he say? He made another circle around the lounge, then turned the corner again.

This time, her chair was empty. Michael walked to the table, staring at the older man.

"Excuse me, sir. Your friend has a telephone call."

The man glanced over his shoulder. "She's gone to the ladies' room."

"Will you ask her to see the hostess when she returns?"

"Certainly."

"Thank you."

Michael strolled on, picking up speed along the way, practically bumping into an attractive young waitress.

"Excuse me, but where is the ladies' room, please?"

"The ladies' room?" she repeated, slightly amused. "To the right there." She pointed.

A narrow hall led past two doors marked LADIES and MEN. Adjacent to the rest rooms, he spotted a pay phone.

Michael moved to the phone, lifting the receiver and pretending to be in conversation.

The door to the ladies' room opened; he waited, ready to question Johnni. A middle-aged woman emerged.

"Excuse me, but there's an urgent phone call for the redhead in the ladies' room. Would you please tell her?"

"Sure." She smiled agreeably and walked back through the door.

Michael held the phone, bracing for the confrontation. The door opened again, and the same woman emerged, shaking her head.

"There's no redhead in there. She must have gone back to her table."

"Thanks." Michael smiled, hanging up the phone. How had he missed her? He had gone one way; she had gone the other. As he gathered his wits and started back to the table, Marty rushed toward him.

"She's leaving."

Michael bolted toward the elevator just as the door closed.

A brass plate over the elevator indicated the location of elevator to floors. The needle angled down to forty-six and stopped. Then the needle moved again, angling to six and stopping.

Just then, the second elevator opened, and Michael rushed on. Punching the button for the forty-sixth floor, he mentally ticked off the seconds until the door opened. Holding the door open with his hand, he stuck his head out and looked up and down the hall. All was quiet. For now, he would assume that someone on forty-six had stepped onto the elevator.

He closed the door and rode down to the sixth floor. He got off and scanned the area. The corridor led to an exit to

Peachtree Road and a glass-enclosed bridge connecting the hotel to a merchandise mart. He spotted her at the entrance to the bridge.

She was walking away from him, walking fast. She wore a tight, long-sleeved black minidress, black hose, and silver high heels.

Michael followed, keeping to posts and plants in case she looked over her shoulder.

She turned a corner.

Michael picked up speed, gaining on her at the glass-enclosed bridge. Through the glass walls he had a view of night lights and Peachtree traffic. The bridge led on to the merchandise mart. He hurried along the corridor, glancing in showcase windows that held mannequins in winter fashion, displays of safari wear, and jewels displayed on black velvet.

Since it was Sunday evening, there were fewer people along the corridor. He imagined that other shops in the merchandise mart would be closed as well. Where was Johnni heading?

He stopped walking and listened. High heels clipped concrete just ahead. He turned down the first corridor, trying to follow the direction of the sound. That corridor led past more shops, which were closed for the evening. She was nowhere in sight.

A second corridor led off, and he turned there. More closed shops—but Johnni seemed to have vanished into thin air. He listened. The clip of heels had stopped. There was an eerie quiet along the front of the closed shops.

Whirling, he ran back to the glass bridge. Automatically, he looked down on Peachtree.

Johnni stood on the corner, flagging a cab.

Michael raced down the corridor and back to the hotel lobby, dodging and colliding with startled people. He jumped on the escalator. Halfway down, he leaped to the bottom floor, trying to ignore the gasps and muffled whispers. Obviously, everyone thought he was a lunatic, or a burglar trying to escape the police. He half expected to be tackled by a security guard.

Back out at the parking deck, he yelled to the valet to grab his car for him. Tossing him the keys, the valet pointed to the Jeep parked right out front. Shoving money into the valet's hand, he leaped into his car and, with a squeal of tires, lunged into the outer lane of traffic. A limo swerved to miss him.

Up ahead, the traffic was clogged with slow evening traffic. A sedan, a sports car, the limo…a taxi!

Michael cut into the passing lane, running a red light, attempting to catch up with the taxi. Just as he paralleled the taxi, he looked into the backseat and faced a party couple in masquerade dress with masks and silver plumes.

Down a side street, he spotted another taxi. All he could do now was chase the closest taxis, and he chose this one. His Jeep two-wheeled the corner, bounced over the curb, and caught up with the taxi.

Intense now, Michael careened toward the taxi, certain Johnni was in this one. The taxi swerved into the other lane as Michael forced his car up beside it.

In the backseat, an elderly couple stared at him, looking terrified by his driving.

He was surrounded by a maze of traffic, but there were no taxis with a redhead in the backseat.

He pounded the steering wheel in frustration, unable to believe she had evaded him again.

Taking a deep breath, he tried to calm the erratic beating of his heart as he turned toward home. He recalled his warning to Tommy.

She's smart as well as dangerous.

~ ~ ~ ~ ~

Later, dragging himself through the front door with thoughts of a cool shower to calm his nerves and wash the perspiration from his body, he caught the red light blinking on his answering machine. He walked over, noted "unavailable" on Caller ID, then pushed the button on his machine.

A sultry voice came on. "Hi, Mr. Detective. I like games, but if you're gonna catch me, you've got a problem. You don't drive fast enough...." This was followed by a sarcastic little laugh...and then the line clicked.

Michael replayed the message, then hurled the phone book across the room before he could control his temper.

Twenty-eight

Monday, October 7

Michael entered the office wearing a five o'clock shadow of a beard. Although his clothing was neat and his hair combed, his eyes held a haggard look. He headed straight for the coffeepot.

"And good morning to you too," Anita called pleasantly.

"Mornin', Anita. Just let me get some caffeine to my brain."

"Is it that bad?"

"Not really. I was out of coffee at home."

Anita laughed. "Then I don't see how you drove to the office without a fender bender. I know your brain doesn't function until you've had a dose of caffeine."

Just then the front door opened slowly. A young man entered.

"Can I help you?" Anita asked.

"Yes, ma'am. I would like to see Mr. Michael Calloway."

Sipping his coffee, Michael studied him over the rim of his large mug. He looked to be in his late twenties, was over six feet tall, about 250 pounds, and dressed in inexpensive gray slacks and a plaid shirt, open at the collar.

"May I give him your name?" Anita asked politely.

"My name is Edwin Allen Holman. I've come to work for you."

"Oh." Anita nodded in comprehension as her eyes turned toward Michael.

"Hi, Edwin." Michael crossed the room, offering his hand. "We're glad to have you working with us." He glanced at Anita. "Is the Xerox machine working okay?"

"It's working just fine."

He looked back at Edwin. "Then you're here just in time to help, Edwin. I have several copies I'll be needing today, Anita. Can you get Edwin started?"

"I'll be glad to," Anita said, leading Edwin over to the machine. She began to explain quite simply how the machine worked, inserting a piece of paper, closing the lid, and pressing a button. A light flashed and a copy rolled out. Edwin looked fascinated.

"I like pictures," he said. "I like to make pictures."

"Good!" Michael called to him. "There'll be lots of pictures to make around here." He took another gulp of coffee, eyeing his desk through the open door. Already there was a stack of phone messages. "Well, I'll leave you two to your work and get busy," Michael called, entering his office.

Closing the door for privacy, he thought that working with Edwin would be good for Anita, who was suffering from the empty-nest syndrome. Anita was a widow. Her daughter lived in Ohio, and her son, still single, had been transferred to California. She had confessed to Michael that it had about killed her to help him pack up and leave, knowing how much she would miss the way he dropped in for meals and for help with his laundry.

She knocked on the door, then entered. "I forgot to tell you that Tommy Kline called first thing. He said the saleslady at Macy's called him last night. She said a woman looking exactly like the sketch Tommy left came in late yesterday afternoon. Bought more purple lipstick, matching fingernail polish, and some very expensive perfume."

"Great job! We're getting warm, Anita."

"Maybe not. Tommy said the salesgirl tried to get the client to start a file, so they could notify her of new products and upcoming sales, but she refused, saying she was planning to move."

"Planning to move?" Michael frowned, scratching his head. What did that mean? Move to where?

He picked up the phone and tried to call Tommy, but all he got was the answering machine. He left a message, then mentally ran through his other options. Hating to bother Tina at work, he nevertheless chose to do so. They had to stay hot on Johnni's trail, if she was planning to leave town.

"Good morning, Michael," Tina answered brightly, after he had gone through another clerk, giving his name and terming the call important.

"Hi. Sorry to bother you. But would you tell Tommy I'd like him to stake out Lennox Mall in his off-hours? I got the message about how our prospective client is planning to move. That may mean she's stocking up on clothes before she departs."

"You want him to cover the entire mall?"

"Just keep a watch. Don't worry, Tina. He seems good at that. He's doing a great job for me. And I'll reward him handsomely."

She laughed softly. "In that case, expect him to hound every shop and vacant bench in the mall."

"Also tell him to keep an eye on the parking lot. We need a description of her car. Ideally, we need the license plates."

She sighed. "You aren't asking much, but I'll get the word to him."

"And tell him we have until Friday to find her. That doesn't give us long."

"Four days to be exact," she answered worriedly.

"We'll do it."

As he hung up, he wondered if he were trying to convince her or himself.

He buzzed Anita. "Got a minute?"

"Sure." She appeared on command, glancing back over her shoulder. "Edwin is so sweet, Michael. I'm glad you hired him."

"Yeah." He glanced toward the open door, hearing the click of the Xerox machine. "Anita, I need your help."

She hiked a brow good-naturedly. "Don't you always? What is it this time?"

He hesitated. "I'll preface my request by telling you we have exactly four days to find a dangerous woman, a woman who has threatened an accident to her twin sister on their birthday, which is Friday. Trust me, Anita. Elizabeth and I both feel she'll carry out the threat."

He finished his coffee and sighed. "Anita, do you remember the car wreck that claimed Dr. Waterford's life? We haven't ruled out the fact that Johnni might have been involved in that accident. We can't afford not to take her threats seriously."

Anita nodded solemnly. "So what is it you want me to do?"

Michael hesitated. He knew he was asking a lot, and he hated to burden Anita with the job.

"Go ahead and say it, Michael, because I'm going to make a deal with you. I'll do this gruesome job, whatever it is. I must admit I can tell by the expression on your face it's a whopper."

"Right. What's your deal?"

"You know I've been wanting to go visit my only son."

202

He nodded, getting the point. "He's in California."

"Right. And I've never been there."

"Which means?"

"Which means I need a little more vacation time to go visit him. What do you think?"

He threw up his hands. "That isn't a deal; it's a pleasure. I'm all for you spending time with your child." He gave her a warm smile. "As soon as we crack this case, start planning your trip, Anita. Call a temporary service and line me up with someone while you're away. But I must warn you: filling your shoes won't be an easy task."

"Oh, Michael, you're a dear! Now what is it you want me to do?"

"Call all the cab companies. Start with the most popular ones. We're looking for the driver who picked up a dazzling redhead in a black dress and silver shoes at the Peachtree Hotel last night around eight-thirty. I'm on my way to the police station, so inform the cab companies that the police are in on this as well. That will inspire them toward closer scrutiny of their records. Tell them he redhead is being brought in for questioning and we expect a full report. Play it to the hilt. You can do it." He winked at Anita.

"Glad for your vote of confidence," she said, shaking her head. Nevertheless, she headed for her dog-eared phone directory.

He grabbed his coat from the rack, glancing across at Edwin, who was carefully making his pictures. Michael sauntered over to him.

"You're doing a good job, Edwin."

The big man smiled. "Thanks. I like to make pictures."

"Well, I'm about to leave."

"Where are you going?" Edwin couldn't seem to resist asking.

"To the police station."

Edwin was obviously impressed. "I've never been to the police station."

Michael hesitated. Might as well invite him. This was pretty routine. "Want to grab your coat and come along with me?"

"Sure!" He looked back at the machine and frowned. "What should I do about my pictures?"

"You can finish these the next day you work."

"That's on Wednesday," he stated proudly. "I work three days a week."

Michael nodded, then motioned to Anita, who was methodically calling cab companies. "Edwin is going with me to the police station. He'll finish his xeroxing on Wednesday."

She nodded, placing her hand over the receiver. "Thank you, Edwin."

"Yes, ma'am. You're welcome."

When they arrived at the police station, Edwin was clearly excited to be accompanying Michael on an important mission. Climbing the steps, they entered a busy center of secretaries and ringing telephones.

"We'd like to see Lieutenant Wilkins," he announced to one woman. Then, spotting the lieutenant behind his glass enclosure, he didn't wait to be announced. Edwin followed, hesitating beside a police officer who was just leaving.

"That's a nice uniform," he said, his eyes full of admiration for the startled policeman.

"Edwin's helping me out," Michael explained with a meaningful look.

The policeman glanced from Michael to Edwin. "Glad you like the uniform, Edwin," the officer replied, then hurried off.

As they entered the office, Michael motioned Edwin to a

chair in the corner. "Hi, Ron," he called to the rumpled-looking lieutenant.

"What's up, Calloway? Got some news for me?"

Ron was stubbing a cigarette butt into an overflowing ashtray. Obviously, he had chosen to ignore any rules about not smoking. One look at Ron confirmed that he ate and slept his job. He was too thin, his eyes were haggard and one of them twitched, and he wore a wrinkled suit that looked as though it had been grabbed from a chair in haste.

"Why are you looking meek, Calloway? It doesn't become you. Oh, I get it!" He shook his head. "What is it you want now? Or more specifically, what do you want from *me?*"

"Ron, I need to check out a Johnni Hankins to see if she has a record. Anywhere. Come on, you have plenty of help who can do that. They only need authority from you. Then it's possible I'll need a stakeout at the Waterford farm just out of Marietta. Who should I contact? I have a couple of guys working for me already, but I need someone who can make an official arrest."

"A quiet little stakeout at the famous doctor's farm above Marietta? You don't want much, do you?"

Michael pulled up a chair and began to explain the situation, starting with Malcomb Waterford's accident, covering the threats by the twin sister and the vandalism, and ending with the death of the father.

"This twin, Johnni Hankins, has promised her sister an *accident* on their next birthday, which, incidentally, is Friday."

"What's your idea of an accident?" Ron lit another filterless cigarette.

"Probably an attempt at murder," he replied, resisting the urge to remind him, again, that he smoked too much. He was here to ask a favor, not aggravate the guy.

Ron frowned, reaching for a pen and pad. "Here's the guy to

see in Marietta. He isn't the pushover I am, I'll tell you in advance."

"Come on, Ron. Never would I, or anyone else, consider you a pushover! The idea is downright comical."

Twenty-nine

As soon as Elizabeth dropped Katie off at school, she headed into the city. She was wearing her red blazer, a navy skirt, and a white silk blouse. She wanted to look official for her meeting with Dr. Waterford's associate, Dr. Phillips.

She frowned vaguely as her Honda joined the line of morning traffic. She was thinking not of the traffic, however, but of the cool and distant voice of Dr. Phillips when she had asked to speak to him about Julie Waterford.

"I'm very busy today," he sighed a bit too heavily, "but I can spare a few minutes around ten-thirty."

"That will be fine," Elizabeth quickly assured him. "I'll look forward to meeting you."

He did not respond in kind, and Elizabeth decided that he was simply not the type who showed his emotions, a habit that became second nature to many therapists, out of necessity.

She had hoped, however, that he would be more enthusiastic at the mention of Julie's name. After all, she was Dr. Waterford's widow. Perhaps he felt Julie should be seeing him, not Elizabeth. She was prepared to be questioned about her credentials, if it came down to that.

The clinic was a quaint, two-story Victorian with dark green shutters and a muted green door. Not a modern building, or even a swank office in a modern complex, she noted, liking the atmosphere. This gave her hope for restoring Oak Shadows. If the renowned Dr. Waterford chose for his clinic a Victorian house in an upscale neighborhood, then she could feel encouraged to continue with her plans for Oak Shadows.

She parked in the rear parking lot, beside several BMWs and a black Mercedes. A couple of less expensive cars were parked on the back row, probably cars belonging to the staff.

She followed the sidewalk paralleling a grassy lawn to the front of the house, climbed the wide steps, and entered, making mental notes with each step. Of course, she didn't, in her wildest dreams, expect to achieve the status of Dr. Waterford, but there was something relaxing about this kind of atmosphere. A swank office was intimidating to many clients. She found this atmosphere reassuring.

A receptionist led the way into Dr. Phillips's office and informed her he would be with her soon.

Elizabeth looked around, impressed. The room was large, with volumes of books stacked on floor-to-ceiling shelves. An expensive-looking desk, probably imported, was the perfect complement to the oriental area rug overlaying gleaming hardwood floors. Framed English hunting scenes were interspersed with the appropriate diplomas, achieving just the right balance between professionalism and quietly stated luxury.

She took the chair facing the desk, a deep red leather chair that seemed to envelop her body upon contact.

The door closed behind her, and she turned slightly to face

a small man, probably in his early fifties, who was regarding her with open curiosity through wireless glasses. He was small and thin with long, uneven features.

"Mrs. Calloway." He nodded to her, speaking in a voice that held a soothing quality.

"Hello, Dr. Phillips."

He sat down behind his desk and studied her momentarily. "How is Julie Waterford?" he asked, although Elizabeth sensed the question was merely a formality. There was no concern in his eyes, or his tone, and this puzzled her.

She explained the situation as quickly and concisely as possible: that Julie was seeing her professionally because she was being stalked by her twin sister, from whom she had been separated since the age of eight.

"I was wondering if Dr. Waterford ever saw Johnni, the sister, professionally, because she seems to have knowledge of him she might not have otherwise."

Dr. Phillips said nothing for a few minutes as he steepled his hands before him and regarded her thoughtfully. "You know the rules of doctor-client privilege, but I will ask my assistant to check his files for..." His voice died as he reached for a pen. "Give me the name again."

As she carefully pronounced Johnni's name, she had the feeling that he was either uninterested or insincere. *Which is it?* she wondered, watching his every move, trying to analyze him.

"If I find anything, I'll let you know."

"Please do," she said, placing her business card before him.

He said nothing more, and the discussion was obviously closed.

"Thanks for your time," she said, coming to her feet.

What time? She didn't like this man. He made her wonder: What was Dr. Waterford really like? And why had he wanted someone like Dr. Phillips as an associate?

~ ~ ~ ~ ~

She left the building, feeling frustrated and confused. Either he wasn't telling her something, or there was nothing to tell. Still, she couldn't shake the feeling he was hiding something from her.

She had planned to meet Dianne Elkins, a schoolmate, for lunch, so she quickened her steps, not wanting to be late. Afterwards, she was going to make a dash by Michael's office to say hello to Anita, and to Michael, if she could catch him there. She was hoping he had made some progress on tracking Johnni down over the weekend, although she doubted that he had since there had been no news from him.

Thirty

Michael and Edwin entered the office, laughing together. Anita, seated at the desk, in conversation with a cab company, pointed toward Michael's office door.

An eyebrow lifted, he could hear female voices drifting through the half-open door, and he walked over, peering inside.

Elizabeth stood beside a tall, dark-haired woman, pointing up to a plaque on the wall.

"...from the Missing Children's Center," Elizabeth explained. "The mayor's son was kidnapped. Little Trey had been gone for three months when Michael took the case. He tracked the grandparents to Canada and brought the little guy home."

The other woman shook her head. "Incredible. You must be very proud of him."

Elizabeth nodded. "I am."

Michael straightened his tie, pleased by the conversation. "Hi," he called pleasantly.

Both women turned to face him.

"Hi, Michael. This is my friend, Dianne Elkins. Dianne, this is Michael."

"Hello, Michael." The woman extended her hand. She looked to be about Elizabeth's age, with striking blue eyes and nice features.

Michael looked back at Elizabeth, and for a moment, their eyes locked and neither spoke.

Dianne cleared her throat. "Well, I know you want to talk to him about a client, so why don't I take a seat out in the reception area and flip through a magazine?"

Elizabeth looked back at her quickly. "Oh, okay, Dianne. I'll just be a minute."

"Take your time." She looked back at Michael and smiled. "It was nice meeting you, Michael."

He nodded. "My pleasure."

Elizabeth crossed her arms and blinked, looking around the room. "You know, I forget how nicely you have this place decorated."

Michael followed her gaze around the room. "Thanks." He walked over to straighten a picture, wondering what was up with Elizabeth.

"Look, I need to talk to you about Julie Waterford."

He turned slowly, saying nothing, motioning her to the chair in front of his desk. Why had he dared hope she would drop by just to have a conversation with him?

"Yeah, I have a few things to add on that subject as well. You go first."

The expression came out of his mouth easily, and for a moment both were swept back to past dinner conversations when they had been eager to share the news of their day. But of course that was before the wedge between them started to widen until the communication had completely ended.

Elizabeth took a deep breath, pushing her thoughts back to the subject at hand as she settled into the chair, crossing her legs.

She related what Julie had told her the day before. "You know, I'm really getting concerned about this situation."

"If you could see what I've witnessed this weekend, you'd be even more concerned."

"Tell me."

He began with the early morning phone call from Johnni, followed by his mad dash to Woodfield and the nursing home.

"The nurses told me Hankins had no family, but that man was their father, I'm sure of it. A redhead had been to see him that morning, one fitting Johnni's description. The nurse said she was someone from an agency in Atlanta. Strange, don't you think, that after she pays him a visit, he has a stroke?"

"And now he's dead," Elizabeth sighed.

"Then, last night, I was sitting at home in the recliner, reading a book, trying to unwind, and I get a call from the hostess at the Sun Dial lounge."

Elizabeth scooted to the edge of her seat. "The Sun Dial?"

"I had shown the sketch of Johnni to the hostess there and asked her to call me if she came back in. Well, Johnni came in last night. Marty, the hostess, called, and I took off over there. I saw her, Elizabeth. She was sitting at a table with an older man whom I suspect she had just picked up. I tried to be casual, but she spotted me and got out of there...."

"So she knows what you look like?"

"Yep, apparently she's been watching me sometime when I wasn't aware of it. I tracked her across the hotel, then lost her. The last time I spotted her, she was getting in a cab in front of the hotel. Anita's spending the day calling cab companies, trying to get a lead on her.

"Oh, one more thing. Last night when I came in there was a taunting little message from her on my answering machine. She let me know she was having fun outsmarting me."

Elizabeth stared into space. "Wow!"

Neither of them spoke for several seconds as they both thought about what was happening. Then Elizabeth focused on Michael again.

"Julie's a wreck. After learning from you that her biological father was in the nursing home in Woodfield, she called and discovered that he died on Saturday."

"Yeah, the ambulance was picking him up when I got there. From what I gathered, he was in very poor health anyway. So is that why she's a wreck?"

"Not the only reason. Johnni called her with some reference to Horn-Rims."

"Horn-Rims?" Michael was puzzled.

"Julie says she's referring to Malcomb Waterford. That he wore reading glasses—you know, the old-fashioned horn-rims."

Michael frowned. "When did Johnni see him?"

"My point exactly. I think Johnni may have been a patient of his. I came into town to meet with his associate, who's about as warm and compassionate as a dead fish. I can't imagine Dr. Waterford working with him. But then," she sighed, "I knew Dr. Waterford only by his reputation as a psychiatrist. I don't know what sort of person he was. Apparently, he was very kind to Julie. The problem is, this Dr. Phillips showed little concern for Julie, and if Johnni has ever been to see either of them professionally, I have my doubts that he'll let me see the file."

Michael leaned back in his chair. "Want me to check it out for you?"

She stared at him for a moment. "How would you do that?"

He grinned. "You don't want to know."

She laughed. "No, I guess not. But we're getting desperate. Julie's birthday is Friday, and I have no doubt now that Johnni will carry out her threat, do you?"

"No doubt at all."

"Anything you get on her will be greatly appreciated. More

than that. It could save Julie's life."

"Consider it done."

Elizabeth stared at him. "You really are amazing at your work."

He hesitated for a moment. When he spoke, his tone had softened. "Thanks for acknowledging that. But then, so are you."

Recalling the book he had been given at the Promise Keepers meeting, he decided to swallow his pride. He was now willing to take the first step toward reconciliation. "Elizabeth, I want to apologize to you for..." He broke off, shaking his head. "Where do I start? I didn't understand the importance of your work, and in retrospect, I think I was more jealous than resentful of your family's money."

She stared at him for a full minute before answering. "Michael, you're being very sweet to say that to me."

He shrugged. "Yeah, well, I've started going to Promise Keepers with Jay. I'm reading one of their books, and I've subscribed to a magazine. I really do want to be a better person, Elizabeth. When I can accomplish that, I hope to be a better father...and husband," he added softly.

His eyes sought hers. How would she react?

She smiled at him. "Speaking of Katie, she'd like to see you. If you can make it, why don't you come up Wednesday night, and I'll prepare that baked mushroom chicken you like. We have a Bible study earlier, but by the time you can drive up from Atlanta we'll be back. Say around seven?"

His smile widened. "You've got yourself a deal. Maybe I'll have that file for you then."

"Perfect." They both laughed, and then suddenly she glanced toward the door. "Oh, I forgot all about Diane. She's been killing time out there for half an hour." She stood up. "Katie's going home with Brooke till I get back; still, I don't want to impose."

Michael walked around the desk and stood beside her. Then, as he stared down at her, something happened between them that neither could have predicted or prevented.

He leaned down, gently planting his lips on hers. "I still love you, Elizabeth. I always will."

Tears filled her eyes. She couldn't speak. She raised on tip-toe to touch her lips to his again. "Me too," she whispered; then she turned and left the room.

Michael smiled after her, suddenly feeling as though he could race through the clouds. He sauntered toward the window and stared up at the sky.

He found himself recalling something his mother had once told him. *"God is rarely early in answering a prayer, but he's never too late."*

"Thank you," he whispered, staring into the clouds.

Thirty-one

M ichael had promised Jay he would attend another small-group meeting of Promise Keepers, and afterwards he left the gathering, humming to himself. He had even signed up to attend a convention next year. It was a wonderful organization. He had swallowed his pride and allowed them to pray for him and his family tonight—a giant step on his part, when it came to dealing with his stubbornness and male pride.

He wondered what the guys would think if they knew he was leaving their reverent gathering to go break into a clinic.

I'm not breaking in, he told himself. *I'm trying to enter legitimately, if it's possible.* He needed a file—a file that just might save a woman's life. Or at least that's what he kept telling himself as he drove slowly down Marshall Drive toward the Waterford Clinic. This was an upscale area in which homes and elite businesses stood together. The Waterford Clinic was located on the same block as a portrait shop and an elite clothing store. The street was well lit, with a large parking lot in back of the clinic.

Michael frowned. Not a place with easy access. The lights were still on within the building. Through the window facing the street, he could see a man running a vacuum cleaner. Turning into the driveway, Michael got out and casually looked around, wondering just what it would take to get a look at Waterford's files.

Michael hesitated on the porch of the two-story gray house, peering into the window. For a moment, he watched the young man, late twenties, slim and agile, busily vacuuming the expensive carpeting. Rock music played in the background as the vacuum droned on.

Michael pecked on the window.

"I need to get in Dr. Waterford's office," he yelled through the windowpane.

The young man frowned, motioning him to the front door. In the meantime, the vacuum cleaner went off.

"Sorry, sir. Didn't hear what you said."

"I'm on an errand for Mrs. Waterford, the widow of the late Dr. Malcomb Waterford. I need to get inside his office for a minute," he stated, trying to sound convincing.

The young man frowned. "I don't know. I'm not supposed to let anyone in. Would you mind if I checked with Dr. Phillips first?"

"Is he still here?" Michael asked.

"No, he's left. It's just that I'm not to let anyone in, no matter what the circumstance. Besides, a new doctor is taking over Dr. Waterford's practice."

"Since someone else is taking over his practice, I don't see any harm in picking up Mrs. Waterford's picture from her husband's office, do you?"

The young man thought it over. "I suppose not. Come on in." The young man unlocked the front door and turned down the volume on the radio.

Michael entered the house where tables gleamed and the chandelier twinkled. This young janitor was obviously good at his work.

"I appreciate it." Michael smiled.

"Yes, sir. I guess you know, Dr. Waterford's office is the last one on the right."

"Yeah, thanks."

Michael hurried down the hall to the last open door and flipped the light switch. A leather chair looked as though it swallowed bodies on contact. It was placed conveniently in front of an impressive desk. The room itself was even more impressive, but Michael didn't linger to look around. He headed straight for a filing cabinet in the corner. Locked.

Glancing over his shoulder, he was relieved to see that the janitor hadn't followed to check on him. Michael removed a key ring, opened a tiny attachment, and fastened the attachment over the lock, pressing. Then he stored the attachment back in his pocket and slipped over to unlock a window. Hoping the janitor wouldn't check the window again, he turned and walked back down the hall.

"Someone already picked up the picture. Thanks anyway," he said.

Several hours later, Michael returned to Marshall Drive. The darkness of midnight was offset by tiny halos of streetlights as Michael's Jeep drove slowly toward the clinic. Glancing around, he noticed that all was quiet as he discreetly turned into the driveway, drove toward the back of the building, and immediately cut his lights.

Michael got out of the Jeep, careful not to slam the door, then walked quickly to the window he had unlocked. The window was situated in a dark, shadowy spot.

He experienced a moment of dread as he pulled on the window. He could only hope the janitor had not been too thorough, and to his relief, he discovered the window was still unlocked.

After climbing through the window, he closed it, drew the blinds, and removed a penlight from his pocket. Following the tiny circle of light, he made his way back to the filing cabinet and withdrew the shiny new key that had been made from his valuable attachment. Once he inserted the key in the lock of the filing cabinet and the lock clicked, he sighed with relief and opened the drawer.

With penlight pointed into the drawer, Michael flipped through the files. He hesitated on one particular file, removed it, and tucked it under his arm. He continued on, checking and rechecking. Then he closed the drawer and headed for the window.

Half an hour later, seated at his kitchen table, he began to read through the file, puzzled. Much of what he read made little sense, but Elizabeth could easily interpret it. He knew one thing, however; he had seen enough to trouble him.

Thirty-two

Tuesday, October 8

To her distress, Katie got up with the sniffles. She did not want to miss school today; the drama class was going to decide on a play for Thanksgiving, and she wanted to participate. She didn't want to hang around the house, and yet she knew she couldn't fool her mom when the sniffles got started. So, at the breakfast table, she delivered the bad news—a sleepless night, a clogged nose, and a funny kind of sore throat.

"Could it be just an allergy?" her mother asked. "Or you may be coming down with a cold. But just to be safe, honey, I think you better stay home this morning and take medicine. If you're feeling better by noon, I'll take you to school."

Katie didn't like the idea, but maybe the medicine would help. And drama class didn't meet until one o'clock anyway.

At precisely eight-thirty, the kitchen phone rang as Elizabeth was pouring a second glass of orange juice for Katie.

She answered it quickly, wondering if Julie might be needing her.

"Hi, Elizabeth."

"Oh, hello, Michael. Your daughter is a bit under the weather. I haven't decided if it's a cold or an allergy, but I'm keeping her home this morning for a dose of medicine. If she improves, she may go to school; if not, there'll be another dose of medicine," she said, grinning at Katie, who was making a face.

"Tell her I'm sorry," Michael answered. "Elizabeth, I have something for you."

"Could it be a file?" she asked, feeling mischievous.

"It is. Only, you need to see it as soon as possible. Unfortunately, I'm in court this morning, but I've called Tommy Kline, the guy who works for me part-time, and he's willing to use a half-day sick leave to deliver the file to you this morning."

"Thank you! Hey, the contents of the file must be important."

"Very important. I don't understand all the psychological jargon, but you will, and we can discuss it as soon as I get out of court. Which reminds me, I've got fifteen minutes to get to the courthouse. Talk to you later."

Elizabeth was still staring at the phone in her hand, wondering what that file could contain. She couldn't wait for Tommy Kline to get here.

"Katie, you rest in your room," she said. "I'm going to hole up in my office this morning."

"What're you doing?" Katie asked, twisting the corner of her Kleenex.

"I'm reading up on some mental disorders. And I'm going to call a friend in Atlanta who specializes in a special mental disorder, one I need to know more about in order to help a client."

"Oh," Katie replied indifferently.

＾＾＾＾＾

At noon, when Michael finished his testimony in court, he returned to the office to check in with Anita.

"Michael, you just had a phone call from a Bessie Abernathy."

Bessie Abernathy...Julie's neighbor up at Woodfield! He turned to stare at Anita. "I'm to call her back?"

"No, she is here in Atlanta. In fact, she's stranded at the bus station."

Michael's stare widened. "You're sure she's here?"

"Yes, Michael." Anita's tone held that threat of irritation that occurred when her efficiency was questioned. "And she left the number of a pay phone at the bus station. She's waiting there."

Michael parked his briefcase and turned back for the door. "Call and tell her I'm on my way, Anita."

The Atlanta bus station was a nest of bedlam. People slept on benches; mothers attempted to keep children corralled; people shuffled in lines, impatiently waiting for tickets.

Michael's eyes swept the crowd until he spotted Bessie seated near a bank of pay phones. She was wearing a thick white sweater over a floral dress, tennis shoes, and socks. On the floor beside her was a scuffed brown suitcase.

"Hi, Bessie," he said as he hurried to her side. "Welcome to Atlanta."

"Oh, Mr. Calloway—"

"Please call me Michael."

"All right, Michael. Bless you for coming. I guess you're surprised to see me."

Michael reached down to pick up her suitcase for her. "I'm just glad you're here. I'll drive you up to Julie's house."

223

Bessie hesitated. "Well, I was going to stay with my niece Belinda, but she's not answering her phone."

"Julie will be glad to see you; I can assure you of that."

"And I'll be glad to see her." She walked slowly along, and Michael realized that she must have a problem with her hip, like many women her age. *Probably arthritis.* He slowed his steps to accommodate her.

"I heard there had been a death at the nursing home," Bessie said. "I got a cousin, Lucinda, who's there, so I called to see about her. But it was Hankins who died."

Michael nodded, standing back for her to go through the front door first. "I know. We learned that." His eyes flew worriedly to his black Jeep, which was parked in a loading zone. "I took a chance on getting a ticket by parking in a no-parking area. Luck must be with us; there's no ticket yet. So maybe we can scoot off before we get caught."

He was trying to be witty, but he could see that Bessie was not in the mood. In fact, she looked quite troubled. Saying nothing more, he opened the passenger's door for her. Then he put her suitcase in the backseat.

His eyes swept the cars around him. This constant over-the-shoulder look was a detective's habit. But he was constantly on the lookout for Johnni now, since she seemed to know who he was.

Michael slammed Bessie's door, hurried around the front of the car, and slid in behind the wheel, locking the doors. With a smooth twist of the wheel, he eased them back into the traffic. Finally he glanced across at Bessie.

She was studying him thoughtfully. "Hankins was the meanest man I ever met," she said, getting right to her point.

"Oh?" Michael was surprised that she was opening up to him so quickly when she had backed away at the mention of Johnni the day he was in Woodfield. He turned back to the traffic. He was glad she had decided to talk. There was no time to waste.

"Yeah, he was in prison for a while," Bessie continued, "but I reckon he got out some time back. So far as I know, he never came up to the old place. Lucinda, that's my cousin, said they found him on a park bench, too sick to stand up."

Michael glanced at her, trying to piece it all together.

"Then welfare took his case, and he ended up in the nursing home. You know the rest of that. But Mr. Calloway, I mean Michael," she corrected with a smile, "there's something I need to tell you about Johnni."

Michael had one eye on the traffic, one eye on Bessie. "Believe me, I'm all ears."

"Well…you see…it was rough on those girls trying to survive with no mother."

The car phone rang, interrupting their conversation. Elizabeth spoke from the other end. "Michael, thank God you sent the file. We have a big problem on our hands."

"Elizabeth, I have Bessie Abernathy in the car with me. She came up on the bus from Woodfield, and I'm bringing her to Julie's house now."

"That's good news. Get here as fast as you can, Michael."

"What's up?" He frowned, pulling the car into the passing lane and turning onto the interstate.

"It's too detailed to go into over the phone. Just get up here with Bessie. Maybe that will help. I'll meet you at Julie's house."

"Be there within thirty minutes. But look, if it isn't safe, don't go there till I phone you back, saying I'm almost there."

"I'll try to wait," she promised, then hung up.

Try to wait? What did that mean?

Michael's concern for Elizabeth increased his speed. He whipped to the outside lane, cutting past cars, swerving back to the inside lane to get around a slow-moving vehicle.

"That was my wife, Elizabeth," he informed Bessie, who was looking puzzled. "She…we have a place near Julie." His words surprised him. *We have a place…*why had he said that? Was God finally moving that barrier in his mind?

"Julie needs a friend. I'm glad she has you folks," Bessie said. "I always felt sorry for those girls. They never had a decent chance. Johnni was a hellion like her old man. Julie was an angel. I came to love her like she was my own. Johnni was another story—she wouldn't let anyone get close to her. Frankly, nobody wanted to."

Michael was listening to Bessie, while one part of his mind raced on to the contents of the file. He thought about what he had read, and now that Tommy had delivered the file to Elizabeth, he could sense her urgency as well. Or had something else happened?

His Jeep tore around the curves, leaving a trail of dust.

"Young man, could you please slow down a little? You'll give me a sick stomach."

"Sorry, Bessie, I don't mean to scare you, and I certainly don't want to make you sick. But that phone call I just had confirmed that Julie's life is in danger and—"

The curve came upon them suddenly.

Thirty-three

For a few terrible seconds, it seemed that Michael would be unable to negotiate the curve in time, but with expert maneuvering, he pulled the Jeep to the left, then the right, then slowly back left again. In the process, he had slowed to half the speed he was making before.

He took a deep breath. If he wrecked the car, he would be of no use to anyone. Then he remembered Julie's answering machine. Forcing himself to calm down, he reached for the small magnetic directory that he tried to keep with him. Opening to the index, he found Julie's telephone number and punched it in.

The telephone rang several times. Then the answering machine came on. Shock filled him at the voice on the other end. It was the sultry voice that had called him, the voice that had led him to Woodfield Nursing Home.

"Sorry," the voice said. "Julie won't be back...."

Mumbling despair under his breath, he tried to call Elizabeth to tell her he was almost there, but there was no answer. Apparently, she had gone on to Julie's house, unable to wait any longer for him.

He had just reached the turnoff to Waterford Farm when Bessie began to retch. "I am so sorry." He hit the attachment to roll all the windows down, hoping some fresh air would help her nausea.

"Believe me, I wouldn't put you through this if it weren't important," Michael told her.

He tore up the drive and parked beside Elizabeth's white Honda. He didn't see the Mercedes, or any other car, for that matter.

The sound of steel guitars and bass drums vibrated over the porch. The front door was standing open.

"Why don't you just sit here till your stomach calms down, Bessie," he suggested as he got out of the car and ran toward the house.

"What's going on?" she called after him.

"I don't know. Just wait."

Michael entered the foyer. Rock music threatened the sound barrier as he looked around the foyer. At his feet, the chandelier was a heap of smashed crystal.

"Elizabeth?" he yelled.

There was no answer.

Thirty-four

P anic broke over him in a cold sweat. "Julie?" he called, sidestepping the mess and heading for the den.

There was no one in the den. Ashtrays overflowed with purple-stained cigarette butts; the air was thick with smoke. Michael winced as he made his way to the stereo and cut the music off. Now, the silence was deafening.

He could feel the danger, smell it, as tangible as the cigarette smoke.

Oh, God, keep Elizabeth safe, he prayed, fighting panic. *I love her; I don't want to go on without her. Please, please.*

He crossed the foyer to the living room. It was a disaster. Broken vases littered the floor; the upholstery on the love seat and chairs had been slashed.

Behind the living room, Michael stared in horror at the dining room. A huge, jagged *J* had been carved in the center of the sleek cherrywood table. Black ink splattered the silver service.

"Elizabeth!" he yelled. There was no answer.

Michael approached the kitchen cautiously. Before him lay a mess of broken dishes. A kitchen knife had been stabbed into the door of a cabinet.

The door to Julie's studio stood ajar. He approached cautiously, keeping his back to the wall. The room was wrecked. Even the glass doors had been smashed. A cold wind blew through the open area, skittering trashed sketches across the floor. The snapshot of Johnni and Julie as little girls was attached to the easel. A black *X* crossed out their faces.

Michael moved back toward the stairwell, looking up. That's where they were; they had to be up there.

"Johnni?" he called gently as he started to climb the stairs. "Johnni, don't hurt Julie. She never meant to hurt you. She loved you." He swallowed hard. "And Elizabeth is a good person. She only wants to help. Don't hurt her." His voice cracked, and he decided it was time to shut up.

He crept down the upper hallway, regaining his composure.

"Let's just talk about this. You don't need to punish anyone. And nobody wants to punish you. You've been punished enough."

The door to the master bedroom was closed. He paused for a moment, hating to draw his weapon, yet knowing that all of his training had taught him to do so. Carefully, he unbuckled his holster and withdrew his gun. He never used the gun, but he did carry it with him on occasion, more as a threat than a weapon.

Pressing his ear against the door, he could hear nothing. He turned the knob slowly, heartsick at what he might discover beyond the closed door.

He forced himself to open the door, his breath jerking through his chest. Fear and concern for Julie were there, but those feelings were swallowed up by his love for Elizabeth.

To his relief, he found no one within the master bedroom. Just more disaster created by a very sick mind. Perfume puddled the carpet; jewelry dangled from bedposts. A purple *J* shimmered on the dresser mirror. On the bed and floor, dresses and blouses had been slashed to ribbons. Pinking sheers were stabbed into the closet door.

He stared at the macabre scene, wondering what such a sick mind might do to his beloved Elizabeth.

From the bedroom, he stepped out onto the verandah, quickly scanning the quiet farm.

The grounds appeared deserted. Through the open door of the garage below, he spotted the back of the Mercedes. He stepped back inside and headed for the steps, taking two at a time.

Michael walked around the pool where sunshine danced pleasantly on the blue water, starkly tranquil in contrast to the surrounding horror.

He stopped walking, then listened. He thought he could hear the sound of a voice, so low it was almost a murmur, coming from the pool house.

Slowly, he crept toward the pool house, slipping toward the door.

"You don't want to do this...." It was Elizabeth's voice. She sounded calm and in control, yet how could she be?

He cocked the gun, and there was silence.

There was the sound of movement, the shuffle of feet.

"NO! PLEASE!" Elizabeth screamed above the sound of a gunshot.

Michael rushed into the room, then came up short, holstering his gun as he took in the scene before him.

Elizabeth was kneeling beside the woman crumpled on the floor; the gun lay inches away. Elizabeth looked bleakly at Michael.

"Oh, darling, I'm so glad you're here."

Michael knelt beside Elizabeth, his arms encircling her shoulders. "I've been worried sick about you."

Then his eyes drifted to the woman Elizabeth cradled, and he stared in dismay.

She was dressed in black spike heels, a black skirt, and a gold silk blouse; red hair cascaded over the pale face. Her eyes were closed.

"She had the gun aimed at her head, but I grabbed her hand. The bullet grazed her shoulder," Elizabeth said shakily.

Michael rushed into the adjoining bath and grabbed a towel, then hurried back and knelt beside Elizabeth. She was brushing Johnni's bangs back from her forehead. Then, her thumb pushed gently at the hairline in the center of her brow. The red moved, revealing dark hair. She pushed the wig back from Julie's head and with a weary sigh removed it.

For a split second, Michael was stunned. Then reality hit him, and he handed her the towel. "Press this against the wound while I call 911."

"The phone is over there." Elizabeth pointed.

Michael turned to the vanity. Beside the telephone he could see the case that held a pair of contact lenses—green lenses, no doubt. A tube of purple lipstick, top removed, sat beside the case. Shaking all thoughts from his head other than getting help for Julie, he quickly dialed 911.

He finished his instructions and hung up the phone.

"The paramedics are on the way."

Elizabeth was cradling Julie's head in her lap as she spoke softly to her.

He could hear Bessie yelling for someone. He had to reassure her. He stepped out of the pool house and found her wandering around the corner of the house, her face filled with concern.

"We're in here, Bessie, but maybe you should just wait. Julie is quite ill. We've called 911."

"Julie…." She pushed past him and rushed inside.

"Bessie, this is my wife, Elizabeth Calloway." Michael caught up. "She's the therapist who was working with Julie."

"Hello, Bessie." Elizabeth smiled sadly, then asked, "When did Johnni die?"

Bessie heaved a sigh. "When the girls were eight. Johnni had pulled one of her pranks. Her daddy slapped her too hard. She fell off the porch and hit her head on a jagged step." Bessie dissolved into tears as she slowly made her way over to kneel beside Julie, who appeared to be in a deep sleep.

"It was the saddest thing I ever saw. The sheriff came and took Hankins off. Little Julie was in shock. She blamed herself for Johnni's death; she felt so responsible for her. But there was nothing she could do."

Michael yanked a Kleenex from the vanity and placed it in Bessie's hand. She wiped at her face. "The social worker came and took Julie away. I heard she got adopted by good folks. I reckon she was happy. Then a few months ago, she came to see me. She was real troubled. Said she had killed her husband."

"Killed her husband?" Michael echoed.

Bessie nodded. "They had a car wreck. Julie was driving. She blamed herself again for another death. That's when all this trouble started. She came up to see me right after the wreck. She told me she was lost again, that she'd married a doctor but he couldn't help her now. She didn't act right. One minute she'd start acting like Johnni, and the next minute she was herself again. I tell you, it was downright scary."

Elizabeth nodded. "I learned this morning that one of Dr. Waterford's specialties was dissociative identity disorder. He was doing a very important book on the subject." Elizabeth took a deep breath. "I think...I hope that he fell in love with Julie." She shook her head. "At least, I want to believe that's what happened, that he wasn't using her as a guinea pig."

"You mean—" Bessie stared at Elizabeth, unable to fathom that a human being would deliberately experiment on a person in such a cruel way.

"We may never know the truth," Michael said.

"When did you learn what was wrong with Julie?" Bessie asked, sniffing.

"Her file was at Waterford's clinic. Michael obtained it for me." She reached forward, closing her hand over his. "There were pages and pages of how Julie took on the personality of her sister, and even her father, to punish herself. Julie Waterford became Johnni in order to satisfy her subconscious, which was burdened with guilt."

Elizabeth paused, taking a deep breath. "I was not experienced enough in dealing with this disorder. For example, I wasn't convinced that a person with one condition, such as agoraphobia, could lose that condition when the dissociative process began. But I was assured this morning by a prominent psychiatrist that this can and does happen. Julie got so much into the role of Johnni that she lost her own identity, with all the problems and drawbacks. She was wild and reckless and unafraid—just as Johnni was. In a strange way, it provided some sort of comfort to her. She was literally coming apart. This is a defense mechanism the mind uses to preserve sanity. I guess it all sounds a bit strange," Elizabeth finished tiredly.

"Those are very wise words," Michael said, looking at her thoughtfully. "And I've never given you enough credit for your hard work. What tipped you off that Julie had this problem?"

"The way she seemed to lose time. Her inability to remember things, and the fact that she seemed to sleep so much. This triggered something I had learned in one of my courses. I was in the process of consulting a friend in Atlanta, but it would have been too late for me to help Julie if not for you, Michael."

Michael squeezed her hand, pleased that somehow the two

of them had prevented Julie's death.

Bessie was shaking her head. "It would have been my fault if she had succeeded with…" Her dark eyes shifted to the gun, and her lips trembled. She turned to Michael. "I should've told you when you came to my house. When you said Julie had hired you to find Johnni, I knew she'd gone off the deep end again. I just hated for her to go back to that hospital and be locked up again. I thought maybe if I talked to her—"

"Don't blame yourself," Elizabeth said kindly. "Guilt is self-destructive. We've just witnessed that."

The scream of an ambulance drew closer.

"And, Bessie, don't worry about the hospital," Elizabeth reassured her. "Naturally, she'll be taken to the hospital in Marietta first, but then I'll have her admitted at Masters and Johnson in New Orleans, where she can get real help for her disorder. She will be treated well, I promise you. But more important, the Master Physician will help in her healing this time."

Bessie nodded. "I tried to talk to those girls about God, but I guess with what they had to live with…"

"This time she'll listen," Elizabeth said, smiling. "I won't give up on her until she does. In the meantime, we're all going to pray for her."

Doors were slamming outside, and Michael rushed for the door. "I'll get the paramedics."

Elizabeth stroked Julie's hair gently. "God, help her," she whispered softly as a tear slipped down Elizabeth's cheek.

Thirty-five

Wednesday, October 9

Michael turned into the driveway leading to Oak Shadows, glancing appreciatively at the towering trees that seemed to envelop him in a glorious canopy of red and gold. This was a beautiful farm, and he had been a stubborn idiot trapped by so much pride that he hadn't seen the beauty—or the blessings.

He began to look at the landscape with new appreciation. Could this possibly be home for Michael Calloway, farm boy from Moonglow?

"You don't deserve all this, Calloway," he said, seeing the lush beauty so in need of care and repair. The work ethic that had been instilled in him through generations of Calloways rose up to taunt him, and he knew it was his father's voice that echoed in his mind when thoughts of a "silver platter" entered his head. His dad was fond of telling stories of people whose money was handed to them on a silver platter, who never did a day's work to earn what they had.

But what had been handed to Elizabeth? True, this was a

glorious estate, but as he had so often reminded her, there was a ton of work to be done.

And then an answer to the problem that had separated them hit him squarely in the face. If he were to share in the enjoyment, could he not also share in the work? That way, he could feel as though he had made a contribution to the contents on the platter.

He smiled to himself, thinking ahead to the upcoming Saturday, his first free Saturday in months. He knew exactly how he wanted to spend that day, and all the free time he could manage in the future.

He pulled his Jeep to a halt in the driveway and reached across for the bouquet of red roses that lay on the seat beside him. He got out, holding the bouquet against his chest and looked down the long avenue of trees. A rather foolish, yet poignant, thought occurred to him. Taking a single rose from the bouquet, he walked slowly down the drive, scattering rose petals here and there along the driveway. Each red petal made a scarlet flash against the pebbles and fallen leaves. It was quite eye-catching, he decided.

"May I ask what you're doing?" Elizabeth called, smiling at him from the porch steps. She stood with her hands on her hips, watching him as though he might be suffering some sort of disorder himself.

"Hi," Michael called out, looking her over.

She was wearing a blue slacks set underneath a lacy white apron. Her hair was pulled back in a ponytail, and with only a light covering of mascara and lip gloss, Michael thought she was the most beautiful woman he knew.

"Yes, you may ask," he replied, dropping one last petal as he returned to the front of the house.

"For you," he said, extending the bouquet. "I assume roses are still your favorite."

"As always." She smiled at him. She was standing on the top

step of the porch, increasing her height by a few inches, so that she stood eye-to-eye with Michael. She reached out for the bouquet, laying her other hand across his shoulder. "Now would you be so kind as to explain what sort of ritual that was?" She inclined her head toward the scattered rose petals.

"Promises," he said, winking at her.

"Promises," she repeated, following the trail of rose petals with her eyes.

"Sometimes we get blown off course, and our promises can get dropped, cast aside, in some cases, lost and forgotten. I haven't forgotten any of the promises I made to you that day at the altar, but I have dropped a few promises." He sighed. "That happens when Calloways get a little too proud or too stubborn. But with faith in God, we keep on following his Word and clinging to our promises, and look where he leads." He threw his hands up, encompassing their surroundings.

Elizabeth sniffed the bouquet and gave a blissful sigh. "Let's go back to the part about the altar, about making promises we both wanted to keep."

She was staring at him with tears welling in her large brown eyes. "I meant every promise I made, and I now know for sure why I fell in love with Michael J. Calloway."

"And I know why I will always love Elizabeth Turner Calloway."

She leaned toward him and their lips met. Then, slowly her arms wound around his neck as their kiss deepened, and he took a step closer, pulling her against his chest.

"What are you two doing?" There was a giggle to Katie's voice as it floated from the doorway.

The two broke apart, drawing a deep breath. "Just saying hello," Michael called to his daughter.

"Yuk, I hope you don't say hello to me like that. Not with Brooke coming."

"Oh?" Michael's eyebrow hiked. "At long last I get to meet your special friend."

"Yep, I'm cleaning my room now," Katie informed him. Then the door banged, and her footsteps echoed down the foyer to the stairs.

"Do you mind?" Elizabeth asked softly. "We were overdue on inviting Brooke over to spend the night, and I must admit to an ulterior motive, as well."

"And just what was your motive?" Michael tilted his head and smiled at Elizabeth, admiring the way the sunshine played over her blonde hair.

"Well—" she sniffed the roses and wrinkled her nose at Michael—"the girls are inseparable. They'll gather up their snacks, hole up in Katie's room for the night, and we'll have the evening mostly to ourselves. We have a lot of talking to do, wouldn't you agree?"

He nodded. "I would."

Laughing, she reached for his hand to lead him inside.

"Elizabeth, wait." He turned to survey the overgrown front yard. "Would you consider it an intrusion if I gave Jay a call and we borrowed a truck and came up to spend the day Saturday? He has a riding lawn mower, and of course I have the electric one. Between the two of us, we could accomplish a lot. Not to mention his knack for trimming hedges. We just might make some real progress here. You know how fast we Calloways work, once we get down to business."

She stared at him for a moment. "An intrusion, did I hear you say? Are you kidding? After meeting with the interior decorator, it'll be all I can do to handle the house. I had decided we'd simply have to ignore the yard for a while."

"Then it's settled."

"But why?" she asked, her brown eyes bewildered.

"Well," he sighed, "because I watched my speedometer and

timed my trip up today, and I can make it in twenty-eight minutes. Less than that from Marietta. Depending on which area of Atlanta one lives in, there's no escaping the interstates or traffic unless you live right next door to work. And few do. I have a lot of friends who spend thirty minutes on the interstate. Furthermore, I've been thinking of moving my office to Marietta, which would really cut my time in half."

"You've been thinking of doing that?" she asked incredulously.

"I'll outline my reasoning later. More importantly, this is a beautiful place, and you're a very lucky woman to have it."

Elizabeth's mouth dropped open. "Did I just hear what I thought I heard, or did my ears play tricks on me?"

"Mind you, I'm not ready to give up the town house. Not yet."

"Nor am I ready for you to give it up," she said, more seriously. "We have some things we'll have to work through, Michael, and it's going to take time. But we're headed in the right direction."

"And I'm agreeable to our going to a marriage counselor, if you want to do that."

Just then the sound of a car on the driveway brought them back to reality, and they turned to see a dark Ford parking behind Michael's Jeep. A little girl hopped out of the front seat, overnight bag in hand, a big smile reflected in her dark brown eyes. She was just about Katie's size, but as dark as Katie was blonde.

"Brooke?" he guessed, glancing at Elizabeth.

"None other."

Just then a woman got out of the car, and Michael caught his breath. She was slim with short red hair, and for one insane moment, he thought he was seeing Johnni.

Elizabeth tapped him on the shoulder. "I know what you're

thinking, but I've become used to the reaction. I see her at school and whenever Brooke and Katie get together. She's a very nice lady."

Michael took a deep breath, seeing as the woman got closer that she was taller than Julie, and more outgoing.

"Hi, there," she called pleasantly. "You must be Michael." She extended her hand.

"Yes, I am. And you're the mother of the little girl Katie never stops talking about."

"It's mutual, I assure you." She looked from Michael to Elizabeth, noting the bouquet of roses. "Beautiful flowers, Elizabeth. Look, is this a good time for Brooke to come? Katie can always come home with us."

"No." Elizabeth and Michael exchanged a mutual smile. "It's a perfect time. In fact, dinner is just now ready. Care to join us?"

"I wouldn't dream of it!" She winked at Elizabeth and grinned mischievously at Michael. "Have a good evening, you two. And I'd say from the load Brooke packed, there'll be plenty to keep the two of them occupied until way past midnight. Still, promise me you won't let them interfere."

Elizabeth promised, then waved good-bye as Brooke's mother headed back to the car.

Watching her go, Michael took another breath. "I wonder how long it will take me to keep my heart from lunging every time I see an attractive redhead with short hair and pretty eyes."

"Not long," Elizabeth said, taking his hand and leading him toward the door. "I intend to see that your mind is filled with visions of a blonde woman who happens to still be your wife!"

Just when it seems that Elizabeth and Michael are back together for keeps, she is involved in a hit-and-run car accident, ending up in the hospital with bruises, cuts, and a concussion. And worse—she has amnesia.

She doesn't remember Michael or Katie or the man behind the wheel who she glimpsed just before the car struck her. When Michael takes her home to Oak Shadows, she is unaware she is being stalked by the driver. As Michael attempts to reconstruct Elizabeth's memory with wonderful times they have shared together, he decides to take her back to the romantic hideaway where they spent their honeymoon. Unfortunately, they are not alone. The stalker has followed them and is just waiting for the chance to erase Elizabeth's memory completely.

Look for *Memories*, second in this series, at your Christian bookstore in May 1998.

Dear Reader,

Thank you so much for being a faithful reader and friend. I cannot tell you how much the cards and letters you send mean to me. I hope you enjoyed *Promises*. The idea for this book came to me in two different ways: first, after hearing the wonderful impact Promise Keepers is having on marriages in trouble, and second, after reading a newspaper article on dissociative identity disorder. After interviewing a therapist who specializes in the treatment of this disorder, I came home armed with books and material. Then one day I met with a woman in Atlanta who graciously consented to be interviewed, hoping her own story might help others who suffer from dissociative identity disorder. This disorder has been kept in the closet far too long because it is often misdiagnosed. The many wonderful therapists who work tirelessly to help patients are to be commended. So also should all the couples who stay together through the ups and downs of marriage because they are committed to the vows, or promises, they made to God and to each other on the day of their wedding.

My prayer for you and yours is that through the help available to those suffering with marital problems or mental disorders, God will lead you to the many people anxious and waiting to help. Most of all, I pray that the Master Physician will heal your every need.

Love, blessings, and prayers to all of you dear people,

Peggy Darty

Watch for the next book in the series,
Memories,
coming May 1998.
Following is a preview of *Memories.*

Elizabeth Calloway steered her white Honda off of Peachtree Road, down a side street to the quaint restaurant where she was meeting Michael. They were planning a quiet dinner before their session with the marriage counselor. She smiled at the warm memories of the reunion she and Michael had had. Turning into the driveway, she noticed the restaurant was less crowded tonight than usual. She drove past the brick wall enclosing the back lot and parked on the front row to watch for Michael.

While she waited, she thought about the lengthy letter she had just received from Julie Waterford's doctors at the clinic in New Orleans. Julie was making great progress, but Elizabeth knew that the Master Physician was at work as well, healing Julie of her disorder.

A screech of brakes interrupted her thoughts as a sleek black Jaguar rounded the back corner of the restaurant. Elizabeth frowned. No one should be speeding like that around a blind corner in the growing darkness. Then there was the sound of another car starting up.

A maroon Ford was heading directly into the path of the Jaguar. Anticipating what was going to happen, Elizabeth jumped out of her car, yelling at the driver to slow down. But her warning came too late. The Jaguar plowed into the Ford with a sickening crunch of metal. Through the window of the Ford, Elizabeth could see a young woman's face contorted with fear as she fought the wheel of the car; the little boy in the front seat lurched back and forth against the seat belt as the car spun around and lunged toward the brick wall.

Elizabeth whirled back to the Jaguar. Above the dash, she met the gaze of a man she knew, only there was something different about him. His eyes held the glaze of one not completely aware of what he had done. Then there was a flash of recognition on his face as he looked at Elizabeth. The engine roared again as the car picked up speed before she could jump back. The fender of the Jaguar caught her right side, tossing her back against the concrete as though she were a rag doll....

As Michael approached the restaurant, he spotted the flashing blue lights of police cars. He parked half a block away and ran down to the restaurant where a yellow ribbon was being stretched across the entrance to the back parking lot. From the gathering onlookers, the familiar face of a policeman emerged. He grabbed Michael's arm and led him around the gawking crowd.

"Thank God, you're here!" the policeman said.

"What's going on?" Michael asked as they turned the corner to the parking lot where two ambulances loaded victims. Then a wave of shock crashed over him as he looked at the woman on the first stretcher—a slim woman whose blonde hair was streaked with blood. Her eyes were closed, her face deathly pale.

"Elizabeth!" He had walked upon many crime scenes in his career as a detective, but he had always been the strong one. Now the woman he loved with all his heart and soul was the victim, and if not for the policeman's strong arm, he would have fainted onto the pavement that was stained with her blood.

Later, Michael would remember the horrible events in a blur: the paramedics hovering over Elizabeth in the back of the ambulance; the driver calling ahead to the nearest hospital as he skillfully maneuvered the speeding ambulance through the six o'clock traffic; Michael in the front seat, physically paralyzed with fear while a million thoughts flew around in his brain...and through it all, the wail of the siren splitting the tranquility of a soft spring night in the suburbs of Atlanta.

PALISADES...PURE ROMANCE

⟶ PALISADES ⟵

Reunion, Karen Ball
Refuge, Lisa Tawn Bergren
Torchlight, Lisa Tawn Bergren
Treasure, Lisa Tawn Bergren
Chosen, Lisa Tawn Bergren
Firestorm, Lisa Tawn Bergren
Surrender, Lynn Bulock
Wise Man's House, Melody Carlson
Arabian Winds, Linda Chaikin
Lions of the Desert, Linda Chaikin
Cherish, Constance Colson
Chase the Dream, Constance Colson
Angel Valley, Peggy Darty
Sundance, Peggy Darty
Moonglow, Peggy Darty
Promises, Peggy Darty
Love Song, Sharon Gillenwater
Antiques, Sharon Gillenwater
Song of the Highlands, Sharon Gillenwater
Texas Tender, Sharon Gillenwater
Secrets, Robin Jones Gunn
Whispers, Robin Jones Gunn
Echoes, Robin Jones Gunn
Sunsets, Robin Jones Gunn
Clouds, Robin Jones Gunn
Coming Home, Barbara Jean Hicks
Snow Swan, Barbara Jean Hicks
Irish Eyes, Annie Jones
Father by Faith, Annie Jones

Glory, Marilyn Kok
Sierra, Shari MacDonald
Forget-Me-Not, Shari MacDonald
Diamonds, Shari MacDonald
Stardust, Shari MacDonald
Westward, Amanda MacLean
Stonehaven, Amanda MacLean
Everlasting, Amanda MacLean
Promise Me the Dawn, Amanda MacLean
Kingdom Come, Amanda MacLean
Betrayed, Lorena McCourtney
Escape, Lorena McCourtney
Dear Silver, Lorena McCourtney
Enough! Gayle Roper
Voyage, Elaine Schulte

⌒ ANTHOLOGIES ⌒
A Christmas Joy, Darty, Gillenwater, MacLean
Mistletoe, Ball, Hicks, McCourtney
A Mother's Love, Bergren, Colson, MacLean
Silver Bells, Bergren, Krause, MacDonald (October, 1997)

THE PALISADES LINE

Look for these new releases at your local bookstore. If the title you seek is not in stock, the store may order you a copy using the ISBN listed.

Surrender, **Lynn Bulock**
ISBN 1-57673-104-9
As a single mom, Cassie Neel works hard to give her children the best she can. This year, young Sarah and Zach want to show their appreciation for what she does by giving her a date with handsome police officer Lee Winter as a birthday present! Surprised and flattered, Cassie accepts. But little does she know where that one date will lead....

Wise Man's House, **Melody Carlson**
ISBN 1-57673-070-0
Kestra McKenzie, a young widow trying to make a new life for herself, thinks she has found the solidity she longs for when she purchases her childhood dream house—a stone mansion on the Oregon Coast. Just as renovations begin, a mysterious stranger moves into her caretaker's cottage—and into her heart.

Moonglow, **Peggy Darty**
ISBN 1-57673-112-X
During the Summer Olympics set in Atlanta, Tracy Kosell comes back to her hometown of Moonglow, Georgia, to investigate the disappearance of a wealthy socialite. She meets up with former schoolmate Jay Calloway, who's one of the detectives assigned to the case. As their attraction grows and the mercury rises, they unwrap a case that isn't as simple as it seemed.

Promises, **Peggy Darty**
ISBN 1-57673-149-9
Elizabeth Calloway, a Christian psychologist, finds herself in over her head when a client tells her about a dangerous twin sister. Elizabeth turns to her detective husband, Michael, asking him to find the woman. Unexpected events plunge the couple into danger, where they rediscover the joy of falling in love.

Texas Tender, Sharon Gillenwater
ISBN 1-57673-111-1
When Shelby Nolan inherits a watermelon farm, she moves from Houston to a small west Texas town. Spotting two elderly men digging holes in her field each night, she turns to neighbor Deputy Sheriff Logan Slade to figure out what's going on. Together they uncover a long-buried robbery and discover the fulfillment of their own dreams.

Clouds, Robin Jones Gunn
ISBN 1-57673-113-8
On a trip to Germany, flight attendant Shelly Graham unexpectedly runs into her old boyfriend, Jonathan Renfield. Since she still cares for him, it's hard for Shelly to hide her hurt when she learns he's engaged. It isn't until she goes to meet friends in Glenbrooke, Oregon, that they meet again—and this time, they're both ready to be honest.

Sunsets, Robin Jones Gunn
ISBN 1-57673-103-0
Alissa Benson loves her job as a travel agent. But when the agency has computer problems, they call in expert Brad Phillips. Alissa can't wait for Brad to fix the computers and leave—he's too blunt for her comfort. So she's more than a little upset when she moves into a duplex and finds out he's her neighbor!

Snow Swan, Barbara Jean Hicks
ISBN 1-57673-107-3
Life hasn't been easy for Toni Ferrier. As an unwed mother and a recovering alcoholic, she doesn't feel worthy of anyone's love. Then she meets Clark McConaughey, who helps her launch her business aboard the sternwheeler Snow Swan. Sparks fly between them, but if Clark finds out the truth about Toni's past, will he still love her?

Irish Eyes, Annie Jones
ISBN 1-57673-108-1
When Julia Reed finds a young boy, who claims to be a leprechaun, camped out under a billboard, she gets drawn into a century-old crime involving a real pot of gold. Interpol agent Cameron O'Dea is trying to solve the crime. In the process, he takes over the homeless shelter that Julia runs, camps out in her neighbor's RV, and generally turns her life upside down!

Father by Faith, Annie Jones
ISBN 1-57673-117-0

Nina Jackson may not know much about ranching, but she knows business. So when she buys a dude ranch and hires recuperating cowboy Clint Cooper as her foreman, she figures she's set. But her son, Alex, doesn't think so. He's been praying for a father, and the moment he sees Clint, he tells everyone that God has answered his prayers and sent him a daddy!

Stardust, Shari MacDonald
ISBN 1-57673-109-X

As a teenager, Gillian Spencer fell in love with astronomy...and with Max Bishop. But after he leaves her heartbroken, she learns to keep her feelings guarded. Now that she's a graduate student studying astronomy, she thinks she has left the past far behind. So when she gets an exciting assignment, she's shocked to learn she's been paired with the now-famous Dr. Maxwell Bishop.

Kingdom Come, Amanda MacLean
ISBN 1-57673-120-0

In 1902, feisty Ivy Rose Clayborne, M.D., returns to her hometown of Kingdom Come to fight the coal mining company that is ravaging the land. She meets an unexpected ally, a man who claims to be a drifter but in reality is Harrison MacKenzie, grandson of the coal mining baron. Together they face the aftermath of betrayal, the fight for justice...and the price of love.

Dear Silver, Lorena McCourtney
ISBN 1-57673-110-3

When Silver Sinclair receives a polite but cold letter from Chris Bentley ending their relationship, she's shocked, since she's never met the man! She confronts Chris about his insensitive attitude toward this other Silver Sinclair, and finds herself becoming friends with a man who's unlike anyone she's ever met.

Enough! Gayle Roper
ISBN 1-57673-185-5

When Molly Gregory gets fed up with her three teenaged children, she announces that she's going on strike. She and her husband Pete stand back and watch as chaos results in their household, in a hilarious experiment that teaches their children how to honor their parents.

A Mother's Love, Bergren, Colson, MacLean
ISBN 1-57673-106-5

By Lisa Tawn Bergren: A widower and his young daughter go to Southern California for vacation, and return with much more than they expected.
By Constance Colson: Cassie Jenson wants her old sweetheart to stay in her memories. But Bruce Foster has other plans.

By Amanda MacLean: A couple is expecting their first baby, and each plans a surprise for the other that doesn't quite turn out as it should.

Silver Bells, Bergren, Krause, MacDonald (October, 1997)
ISBN 1-57673-119-7

By Lisa Tawn Bergren: Noel Stevens has to work up the ranks in her new job, but being assigned to Santa's workshop is too much. Until she gets to know Santa....

By Laura Krause: Christian novelist Bridger Deans goes to spend Christmas with her family and finds her ex-fiancé there.

By Shari MacDonald: Madison Pierce feels lonely at the thought of her best friend's wedding...until she meets the best man.

Our new line:
ALABASTER BOOKS
Romance, mystery, comedy....Real life.

Homeward, Melody Carlson
ISBN 1-57673-029-8

When Meg Lancaster learns that her grandmother is dying, she returns to the small town on the Oregon coast where she spent vacations as a child. After being away for twenty years, the town hasn't changed...but her family has. Meg struggles with her memories of the past and what is now reality, until tragedy strikes the family and she must learn to face the future.

Arabian Winds, Linda Chaikin
ISBN 1-57673-3-105-7

World War I is breaking upon the deserts of Arabia in 1914. Young nurse Allison Wescott is on holiday with an archaeological club, but a murder interrupts her plans, and a mysterious officer keeps turning up wherever she goes!

Lions of the Desert, Linda Chaikin (October, 1997)
ISBN 1-57673-114-6

In 1915, Allison Wescott arrives in Cairo to serve the British military and once again encounters the mysterious Bret Holden. And to mix things up even further, the chaplain she is thinking of marrying comes to Cairo as well.

Watch for the final book in the trilogy, coming in spring 1998!

Chase the Dream, Constance Colson
ISBN 0-88070-928-6

After years apart, four friends are reunited through the competitive world of professional rodeo, where they seek fame, fortune, faith…and love.

Song of the Highlands, Sharon Gillenwater
ISBN 1-57673-946-4

Kiernan returns from the Napoleonic wars to find out he's inherited a title. At his run-down estate, he meets the beautiful Mariah, and finds himself swept up in the romance and deception of a London Season.

Watch for more books in Sharon Gillenwater's Scottish series!

Promise Me the Dawn, Amanda MacLean
ISBN 0-88070-955-3

Molly Quinn and Zach MacAlister come from very different backgrounds, but both seek to overcome the past. Enduring hardship and prosperity, the promise of a meeting at dawn brings them through it all.

Redeeming Love, Francine Rivers
ISBN 1-57673-186-3

The only men Angel has ever known have betrayed her. When she meets Michael Hosea in the gold country of California, she has no reason to believe he's any different. But Michael is different. And through him Angel learns what love really means—the kind of love that can wipe away the shame of her past.